O9-BUA-381

BUILDING SERMONS
TO MEET
PEOPLE'S NEEDS

Harold T. Bryson
James C. Taylor

BROADMAN PRESS
Nashville, Tennessee

Unless otherwise indicated, Scripture quotations are from the King James Version of the Bible.

Scripture quotations marked (RSV) are from the Revised Standard Version of the Bible, copyrighted 1946, 1952, © 1971, 1973.

Scripture quotations marked (NIV) are from the HOLY BIBLE *New International Version,* copyright © 1978, New York Bible Society. Used by permission.

© Copyright 1980 • Broadman Press.
All rights reserved.

4221-09
ISBN: 0-8054-2109-2

Dewey Decimal Classification: 251
Subject headings: PREACHING//SERMONS

Library of Congress Catalog Card Number: 78-74962
Printed in the United States of America

Contents

Introduction 7

1. Building Sermons: An Overview.......... 11

The Preacher—Thinking about self—Thinking
about God—Thinking about the Bible
The Listeners—Learning about your listeners—
Loving your listeners—Feeding your listeners
The Sermon—Building your own sermon—
Considering one sermon-building method

2. Studying the Bible for Building the
   Sermon........................... 22

The Historical Perspective—An understanding of
Bible history—An understanding of the biblical
world—An example of background material
The Analytical Perspective—An understanding of
textual analysis—An example of textual analysis
The Exegetical Perspective—An understanding of
biblical literature—An understanding of biblical
language—An example of exegetical work

3. Putting People in Sermons.............. 38

Preaching from a Person—The introspection of the
preacher—The preacher's observation of life—
The visitation of the preacher
Preaching to People's Needs—The awareness of
human needs—The understanding of human
stages—The discerning of personal problems—
The helping with life's crises—The support for
life's relationships

Preaching with Persons—The connection of the preacher with the audience—The connection of the text with the audience—The connection of sermon form with the audience

4. Focusing on One Sermon Idea............52

The Relationship of Sermon Idea and Text—From the Bible to idea—From idea to the Bible

The Anatony of a Sermon Idea—An overview of the sermon idea—The naming of the sermon idea—The example of a one-idea sermon

The Essence of the Text—The text studied—The text summarized—The examples of ETS

The Proposition of the Sermon (ESS)—The necessity of a proposition—The qualities of a proposition—The types of propositions—The examples of propositions

5. Directing the Sermon Idea to Action 69

The General Purposes of Preaching—The evangelistic purpose—The growth purpose—The relational purpose—The therapeutic purpose

The Different Domains of the Sermon—The cognitive domain: knowledge—The affective domain: emotion—The psychomotor domain: action

The Specific Sermon Objective—The concept of an objective—The qualities of an objective—The importance of an objective—The examples of objectives

6. Developing the Sermon 81

Probing the Proposition—The probing questions—The one question—The unifying word

Unfolding the Proposition—The mechanics of major divisions—The qualities of major divisions—The examples of major divisions

Expanding the Proposition—The use of substance material—The use of illustrative material

7. **Introducing, Concluding, and Putting Transitions in the Sermon** 103

Introducing the Sermon—The purposes of an introduction—The qualities of an introduction—The interrelated segments of an introduction—An example of an introduction

Concluding the Sermon—The purposes of the conclusion—The qualities of the conclusion—The interrelated segments of the conclusion—An example of conclusions

Putting Transitions in the Sermon—The values of transitions—The types of transitions—The examples of transitions

8. **Communicating the Sermon** 117

The Concept of Communication—The definition of communication—The factors in communication

The Preparation for Communication—The preparation of the preacher—The preparation of the sermon

The Preacher as Communicator—The preacher's self-communication—The preacher's vocal communication—The preacher's visual communication

Conclusion 134

Bibliography 136

Harold T. Bryson
to
Judy Bryson
My wife, who is my best friend
and my favorite listener

James C. Taylor
to
"Maidee" Wilkins Taylor
My wife, my friend, my helper

Harold T. Bryson and James C. Taylor
to
Our students

Introduction

The origin of this book has kinship with the merging of two rivers. Two rivers existed side by side. One had flowed longer than the other river. It had received the water and rich deposits of rivers, creeks, and streams. The other river was formed later. The two rivers existed separately, but ultimately they merged. The water from the older river mixed with the younger river. Their waters became intermingled. As they flowed together, their waters blended thoroughly. Other tributaries flowed into the combined river, and this one river was filled with deposits from many sources. As the river flowed, it emptied its waters in a large gulf. If you looked at the river, you could not tell what water belonged to what river.

This analogy fits the formation of this book. James C. Taylor resembles the description of the river which existed longer. He has been a pastor, a navy chaplain, and a seminary professor. He has taught preachers to build sermons for over three decades. Through these decades many streams of homiletical information flowed into his life and ministry—Charles W. Koller, George Buttrick, Andrew W. Blackwood, H. Grady Davis, John A. Broadus, Austin Phelps, Phillips Brooks, Halford Luccock, Ralph Sockman, and others. Students from several generations have learned from this teacher of preaching. They have observed the character of his life, and they have applied his techniques of building a ser-

mon. Also, he has listened to their feedback; thus, he
has been able to improve his content and method of
teaching continuously.

The other river in the analogy is Harold T. Bryson.
His system of preaching was influenced by Taylor in an
expository preaching class. Bryson listened to Taylor's
theory of preaching and applied it in his student pastorate and in subsequent pastorates. He sought each week
to build sermons with the idea of helping his people,
according to the system shared by Taylor. Bryson
served as a pastor for nineteen years. The mechanics of
"building" a sermon to meet people's needs intrigued
both men. Bryson, in the pastorate, and Taylor, in the
seminary, shared ideas with each other. They listened to
each other. They learned together about one system of
building a sermon. They continuously insisted that the
system of sermon construction must be subservient to
helping people with their needs.

The two lives merged in 1976 with joint vocational
responsibilities. Bryson became a teacher of preaching
with Taylor at the New Orleans Baptist Theological
Seminary. They continued to define and to make practical their system of sermon building which emphasized
an ETS (essence of the text in a sentence), a proposition,
a probing question, major divisions, and other matters.
Tributaries of student insight flowed into their thinking.
Requests came for the Taylor-Bryson system of sermon
construction to be written. This book is the result of
those requests.

As you read and study this book, you will detect deposits of information from many sources. Identifying
Taylor's contribution and detecting Bryson's input
would be like identifying the separate waters of two
rivers which have merged. Some will observe the distinctive influence of Taylor. Others will see the contribution of Bryson. The two men worked together on this
book. They have listened to students who used the sys-

tem week after week in their pastorates. They have read numerous books on preaching. Separating the contributions of students, homilists, pastors, and doctoral students is impossible. This book has taken on many deposits, and now it flows to a wider gulf.

Purpose of the book. This book has one major objective—to help you build sermons to meet people's needs. You will need to study the Bible, to study the needs of people, and to bring these two matters together in sermon construction.

Definition of terms. Before you start reading the book we want to define some terms.

Text—The portion of Scripture chosen as the foundation of the sermon.

Background Material—A compilation of historical facts that relate to the text.

Analysis—A skeleton passage of Scripture which discloses clearly the structure and progression of thought.

Exegetical Work—A study of words, phrases, and the grammatical relationships in a passage.

Essence of a Text in a Sentence (ETS)—A simple sentence which states a truth of the text.

Proposition (ESS)—A simple sentence which states the essence of a sermon in a sentence

Objective—A statement of what the preacher hopes to accomplish in the lives of the hearers.

Probing Question—A question put to the proposition in order to determine a unifying word and to get major divisions.

Unifying Word—A plural noun which assures unity of the major divisions of the sermon.

Transitional Sentence—A sentence used between the introduction and sermon body which incorporates the unifying word.

Major Divisions—The outline of the sermon which emerges from the proposition.

Substance Material—The expansion of the major divisions.

Special Acknowledgments. We have many people to thank for the completion of the book. Our wives, Maidee and Judy, tolerated our absences, listened to our writings, and understood us when we had been too long at the desk with the pen.

We want to express appreciation to our students. Without them we would not have written the book. They have listened to our thoughts, tried our methods, questioned our conclusions and our thinking. We could never express enough gratitude for these God-called persons who want to learn how to build sermons in order to meet people's needs.

A word of appreciation also goes to Miss Pat Engle who typed the rough draft of the manuscript. We also want to thank Miss Kathryn Harper for typing the final copy.

1
Building Sermons: An Overview

Before attempting a major project of construction, a person should give serious thought to what he is going to do. Maybe you have discovered firsthand that it is better to read and to think about the instructions before attempting to assemble a gymnasium set or a toy you purchased for your child. Thinking about the task first would be better than having to disassemble it and do it over because you omitted a part or made a wrong connection.

Jesus Christ spoke about serious thinking. He challenged potential disciples to think seriously about initial commitment to him. "For which of you, desiring to build a tower, does not first sit down and count the cost, whether he has enough to complete it?" (Luke 14:28, RSV). After giving general exhortation to friends in Philippi, Paul spelled out several good things for them and challenged them to "think about these things" (Phil. 4:8, RSV). Rather than doing and then thinking, you would profit by thinking before doing. There is abundant scriptural support for giving thought before taking action.

Before attempting to build a sermon, you might need to think generally about the task. You are not just to build sermons; you are to build sermons that meet the needs of people. Thinking about the task before you get to the actual construction might save you time and anxiety later. What you think about the task of building sermons will determine what you do about it and how well you do it.

The title of this book suggests a threefold emphasis. The three emphases are: (1) the preacher—the builder of sermons; (2) the listeners—the receiver for the sermons; and (3) the sermon—the product of the builder's work. An understanding of these interrelated components is essential if you are to receive much help from this book.

The Preacher

Building sermons isn't all that a pastor-preacher does, but it's one of his primary responsibilities and privileges. Building and delivering sermons relates to the total life and ministry of a pastor. In order for a sermon to come into existence, a person must design and build it. The quality of a sermon rests largely upon the builder's character, skill, and patient commitment to the task. Joseph Parker, a London pastor in the latter part of the nineteenth century, said that the most important part of a sermon was the man behind it. Think then of the builder before you think of the sermon. In thinking of the preacher, the builder of sermons, we pose three crucial questions: What do you think of yourself as a person? What do you think of God? What do you think about the Bible?

Thinking about self. The first question is, What do you think of yourself as a person? You should think of yourself as a unique person. No one else in the world is exactly like you. No two people are alike. God does not call just one type of person to build sermons. He calls people with diverse personalities, abilities, and skills. Therefore, God's call is not to copy someone else. It is a call to recognize your gifts, your strengths, and your weaknesses. It is a call to be the self that you are.

How you *see* yourself is important. Over the years we have observed contrasting opinions that young people have of themselves. Some young people think negatively of themselves. This kind of image leads to serious personality problems and to difficulties in interpersonal relationships. Others seem to have an exalted opinion of themselves which leads to haughty arrogance and to false pride. Fortunately, most builders of sermons have not chosen either of these alternatives. They have chosen a healthy self-image. This self-image results from acknowledging their uniqueness as a creation of God and from confessing their rebellion against God and their human fallibility.

Having a healthy self-image helps the builder of sermons. It gives a degree of comfort with yourself. You can honestly say, "This is who I am. I shall start with who I am and seek to grow and to actualize the unique personality which God has given me." A healthy self-image also gives a reasonable confidence in yourself as a person and in your ability with God's help to communicate the Christian message. Furthermore, a good self-image helps you to think in the realm of possibility. Thinking well of yourself, according to the biblical view, enables you to maintain a compassionate heart toward others, a determination to grow continuously mentally and spiritually, and to keep a healthy body.

Thinking about God. A second question that the sermon builder needs to face is, What do you think about God in relation to the building of sermons? What does God have to do with building sermons? Is sermon building just a human craft? Leaving God out of the sermon-building process would reduce preaching to humanistic speech making. The building and delivery of a sermon has both a human and divine dynamic. You must not leave out the divine dynamic.

God helps the builder of sermons. He leads the builder to insights for messages. With his Holy Spirit, God leads the builder to know what to build. "But the Counselor, the Holy Spirit, whom the Father will send in my name, he will teach you all things, and bring to your remembrance all that I have said to you" (John 14:26, RSV). Getting a sermon idea and structuring the idea does not rest solely upon the builder. God is involved intimately in the process.

God also helps in many other ways. The preacher's daily communion with God enhances preaching. When God called Joshua to lead Israel after the death of Moses, the Lord promised that he would be with Joshua. The Lord further instructed him to be strong and to be of good courage. The only way Joshua could lead was to live day by day with the assurance that God would be with him (cf. Josh. 1:9). The apostles not only heard the Lord's command in the Great Commission but they also heard his promise to be with them always (cf. Matt. 28:19-20). A great preacher and teacher of homiletics said: "In my judgment, the preaching that fails today fails because it is not grounded in a deep devotional life on the part of the preacher."[1]

In thinking about God, you need to consider what God wants to do with a sermon. God intends that sermons be built to help people with their needs. The best preachers are those who think that God wants to help people by means of their sermons. Paul was anxious to preach in Rome. "So I am eager to preach the gospel to you also who are in Rome" (Rom. 1:15, RSV). He believed the Romans had many needs, and the Christian gospel could meet those needs.

The measure of your ability as a preacher will be strengthened or weakened according to your communion with God and according to your confidence in what God wants to accomplish in a sermon. So, think seriously about God. Leaving God out would mean that you would have to reassemble your sermon. Preaching will never "work" without God.

Thinking about the Bible. We have posed two serious questions, but we want to ask some more. What do you think about the Bible? Does the Bible have an important place in your life? Do you consider the Bible as God's inspired, authoritative Word for you? Do you think the Bible will furnish helpful ideas for your sermons? Of course, what you think about the Bible will not change what the Bible is. However, what you think about the Bible will determine the person you become, the kind of sermons you build, and the kind of help you give your people.

In thinking seriously about the Bible, you soon conclude that it is not an encyclopedia of religious information or a collection of moral maxims. It is a holy history of God visiting, speaking, leading, judging, and helping people. God's Word in ancient days helped people in different life situations. The Bible has been uniquely inspired, marvelously preserved, and thoroughly proven. You will need to adopt the Bible as your authoritative foundation for messages to your people. Through the centuries preachers have read and studied God's Word, then they preached messages on the Bible to meet the needs of people. When Paul spoke to young Timothy about his pastoral responsibilities, he said, "I charge you in the presence of God and of Christ Jesus who is to judge the living and the dead, and by his appearing and his kingdom: preach the word, be urgent in season and out of season, convince, rebuke, and exhort, be unfailing in patience and in teaching" (2 Tim. 4:1-2, RSV). Resolve to study carefully the Bible so that the foundation for your sermons will be a word from God rather than a human opinion.

The place to begin thinking about building the sermon is with the builder. If you were going to build a house, the quality of the house would be determined greatly by the character and skill of the builder. You need to think of yourself as a builder of sermons to meet people's needs. The task requires your best, but it is too big for you alone. God will help you, for he wants to help others through your sermon. He has provided his Word for an authoritative message, and he has provided his Holy Spirit to guide and strengthen you for the task.

The Listeners

Now that we have thought about you, the builder of sermons, we come to think about the listeners, the receivers of sermons. In your thinking about building a sermon, you cannot consider only the preacher and the sermon. You must consider those who listen to the sermon. The kind of person you are will determine your thinking about people. What you think about people will be a vital factor in building sermons to meet their needs. To engage in thoughts about the listeners, we submit three questions: Do I seek to know the people to whom I preach? Do I really love people? and Do I seek to feed the people spiritually with my sermons?

Learning about your listeners. The first questions worthy of consideration are, Do I seek to know the people to whom I preach? Is there a vital connection between knowing people and preaching to them? The answers to these questions are obvious. Knowing your listeners will enhance your ability to communicate and to help them with their diverse needs. You might need to know each member by name. One pastor of a church in excess of two thousand members claims that he knows each member by name. Of course, learning about your listeners will involve much more than knowing their names. It will involve the knowledge of their needs. You need to know your people and their problems with sin, frustration, fear, hate, sorrows, discouragement, disappointment, and anxiety. You will also want to know their hopes, joys, loves, and victories. Preaching will be more effective when you understand your listeners.

You can learn about your listeners by making a study of human beings in the Bible. As you read and study

Bible characters and biblical concepts, you confront people with their problems and with their possibilities. Studying psychology will also enhance your biblical understanding of human beings. Visiting with people substantiates and personalizes your study in the Bible and in psychology. Ezekiel was able to preach to the needs of the Israelites in the land of Babylon because he visited with them. "The Spirit then lifted me up and took me away, and I went in bitterness and in the anger of my spirit, with the strong hand of the Lord upon me. I came to the exiles who lived at Tel Aviv near the Kebar River. And there, where they were living, I sat among them for seven days—overwhelmed" (Ezek. 3:14-15, NIV). Jesus helped people because he went to Judea, Samaria, and Galilee, and encountered people in real-life situations.

You cannot afford to shut your eyes to people's needs. A woman upon returning from a walk in the woods was asked by Helen Keller what she saw. The woman replied, "Nothing in particular." In relating the woman's remark to a friend, Helen Keller said that she had learned that "seeing people see little." What do you see in your people? Think about developing the observant eye and the attentive ear of people's needs.

Loving your listeners. The next questions worthy of consideration are, Do you love people? Is one reason you preach to help people out of a genuine love for them? You will be a better builder and communicator to people when you love your listeners. Think of the great preachers in Bible times—Jesus, Peter, Paul. They had an immeasurable love for their listeners. Even though listeners disagreed, opposed, and even sought to kill these preachers, they continued to love. People listen better when they detect someone who cares for them and seeks to help because he loves them.

James Stalker, a British pastor at the turn of the twentieth century, related a personal experience in his book *The Preacher and His Models.* In his first pastorate he learned something that no preacher or educator had conveyed to him. He fell in love with his congregation. He said that loving his congregation was the secret of his happy and successful ministry.

Once a young preacher discussed his pastoral difficulties with a denominational leader. As the discussion progressed, he confessed: "My real problem is that I don't care for my people." Can you imagine a greater problem than the failure to love your listeners? You may have many assets for preaching, but nothing would be strong enough to counteract the lack of loving your people.

A layman once said to young preachers, "If you want to narrow the gap between the layman and the preachers, then love them. Have a compassionate heart toward them." You may be a multi-talented person, but if you love books and study, administration and organization, speaking or lecturing more than you love people, you will never reach your potential as a preacher. Loving people means that you will seek their highest good for the glory of God.

Feeding your listeners. With the other questions pondered we now ask, Do I seek to feed the people spiritually with my sermons? Do I seek to give people life support with my sermons? Do I seek to help people with their needs? After giving Simon Peter the love test, Jesus gave him the command, "Feed my sheep" (John 21:17).

People hunger and need the Bread of life. They yearn for sermons to help them with the problems, decisions, opportunities, crises, and other issues of life. God has chosen you as his instrument through whom he wants to work in order that people may be fed. Good cooks work hard to make their meals appetizing and palatable. Likewise, God-called preachers should give diligent attention to making their sermons attractive and nourishing for the lives of people.

The Sermon

You have been asked to think about the preacher and the listeners. Now we want you to think about the sermon itself. No sermon exists in isolation. It relates to the preacher, for it is his product. It relates to the people, for it will be built with them in mind. To do some preliminary thinking on the sermon, two questions might be applicable: Can I build my own sermon? and Do I need to give consideration to a method of building sermons?

Building your own sermon. Deep within most preacher's minds is the question, Can I build my own sermon? Most beginning preachers admit their first sermon building came as a result of copying what another preacher had said or written. Though this may be acceptable in the very early stages of preaching, you must move to a place where you build your own sermons from the Bible and direct them to the needs of people. One pastor of a rather large church, who graduated from an accredited theological seminary, confessed that he had used other preachers' sermons so long that he could not build his own. He said that his guilt became so intense that he decided that he either had to build his own sermons or to give up the pastorate. He soon left the pastoral ministry. Another pastor of a similar circumstance—pastor of a large church, graduate of a seminary, and copier of other preacher's sermons—decided that with God's help and with professional guidance he could build his own sermons. He stayed at his church, and his people noticed a change in his sermons.

You will feel better about your preaching when you develop your system of building a sermon. Building sermons week after week comprises one of the most demanding duties of a pastor. You need some organized system of arranging your ideas. Looking back each week at the previous Sunday's sermon and knowing it was built by you will bring a great feeling of joy and accomplishment to your preaching.

Considering one sermon-building method. If you want to learn one method of sermon building, ask yourself these questions. Do I need to give serious consideration to the sermon-building method of this book? Will it help my communication of a sermon if I learn this sermon-building method? Will my people be helped if I arrange my sermons better? No doubt many do not find joy in sermon building because they have not found a workable method. Approaches to sermon building will differ. No two preachers are alike. Nonetheless, whatever method of sermon building you choose, the essential ingredients of yourself, God's Word, and your listeners ought to be in it. Leaving out any ingredient would be like leaving out a necessary part of a recipe. Put yourself, God's Word, and your people into the sermon. Once some children watched an artist painting. After a while one of the children said, "Mister, please put us in the picture." Your people and your God ask, "Put me in your sermon."

In this book we present one approach to building sermons. It is not the only method. It is a system where we seek to arrange a biblical idea in the light of people's needs. We invite you to study the guidelines offered. Hopefully, you will experience the joy which we have received in building sermons from the Bible with the needs of people in mind.

Think briefly about this method. Every sermon begins with an idea. This idea relates to the Bible and to the needs of people. You will summarize your text, project the essence of the sermon, and state an objective in the early beginnings of sermon preparation.

Your sermon idea needs structure. Leonardo da Vinci said that in painting you start with bones, then muscles, and finally the flesh. He said that you show the painting so that the muscles may be seen. Likewise, you start with basic structural principles in a sermon so that your listeners may hear and heed the message God has given you. You will want your sermon to be free of vagueness, ambiguity, and indefiniteness. We ask you to follow carefully the guidelines in this book for building and communicating a sermon. In the remaining chapters, we shall explain, discuss, amplify, and illustrate our method of building a sermon. From this method you may adopt and adjust to make your own method. We have confidence that putting the method into practice will give you joy as you build your own sermons to meet the needs of your people.

Note

1. G. Earl Guinn, "A Professor of Homiletics Talks About Preaching," *Proclaim* (July-August-September, 1979). Vol. 9, p. 3.

2
Studying the Bible
for Building the Sermon

Preaching that meets the needs of people gives a central place to Bible study. Christian faith rests on the Bible as the normative guide. In the Old Testament you will find the background for the Christian faith, and in the New Testament you will find the fullest expression of the radically new faith and life that Jesus Christ brought to the world. To preach authentic biblical sermons which meet people's needs, you must inevitably take your stance as a conscientious interpreter of the Bible.

Interpreting the text for a sermon relates directly to the issues of life. Of course you need to develop skills in Bible study in order to interpret the Bible — learn biblical languages, study Bible history, master grammatical and theological aspects of the text, buttress understanding with geographical, political, economic, and social conditions of the biblical world, and use other principles of interpretation. To deal solely with hermeneutical (science of biblical interpretation) matters might cause you to miss the life dimension of your text. Your whole system of studying the Bible for a sermon is brought to bear upon the task of interpreting life. You study the Bible with the best hermeneutical skills in order to help people reconcile broken relationships, rectify injustices, forgive guilts, find the meaning of life, conquer pain, heal grief, face death victoriously, and face other areas of need. Christian preaching can only help people with

22

these needs after careful and diligent interpretation of the biblical message.

Studying the text constitutes a crucial process for the building of the sermon. You will need to work hard to understand the text for yourself in order to make it understandable for your hearers. The text existed in an ancient language that had to be translated. It happened in a period of history unlike ours, and it occurred amid a different culture. Many customs, world views, and other matters of the text are quite vague to people in today's world. Consequently, you must study the text to understand what God said through ancient writers. You will study what the text *meant* so that you may convey what the text *means*. The same Holy Spirit who inspired the original writing will aid you in understanding, applying, and sharing the truths of the text. Studying the Bible for the purpose of building the sermon will be viewed from the historical perspective, the analytical perspective, and the exegetical perspective.

The Historical Perspective

The Bible is primarily a book of events. Both the Old Testament and the New Testament are set in the framework of historical events. The central event is the life, death, and resurrection of Jesus. Every book of the Bible needs to be studied in the context of a particular historical period and in the various circumstances which surround that period of Bible history.

An understanding of Bible history. The Bible originated in a historical way, and it can be understood only in the light of history. The events in each book of the Bible came out of a time in history. A text can only be understood accurately and completely when the historical perspective has been studied. In some way you will need to get out of the twentieth-century environment and identify as closely as possible with the life and feelings of biblical times. Studying a text from its historical perspective means that you will seek to understand the life situation which is recorded in the text.

To understand the life situation of a text, you need to place the particular biblical book within its historical context. This would mean a study of the particular period of Bible history. Many Old Testament and New Testament scholars list thirteen periods of Bible history: (1) Period of Beginnings, (2) Period of the Patriarchs, (3) Period of the Exodus and Wilderness Wanderings, (4) Period of the Conquest, (5) Period of the Judges, (6) Period of the Kingdom, (7) Period of the Two Kingdoms, (8) Period of Judah Alone, (9) Period of the Captivity, (10) Period of the Restoration, (11) Period Between the Testaments, (12) Period of Jesus' Life and Ministry, and (13) Period of Early Church. Because the unique truth of God's nature and his dealing with human beings are bound up in the events of biblical history, they can best be disclosed when you enter into the historical event with a degree of understanding. For example, if you selected a passage in Ezekiel as a text, you would need to associate Ezekiel with the Period of the Captivity. Putting the book and text in its particular period of Bible history helps you know what God meant when he spoke at that time.

In some instances you need to know more than one period of Bible history for a text. The events recorded in the book might have occurred at one time, but they were recorded at another time. For example, the events in the gospel according to Mark happened somewhere in the years AD 5-33 (Jesus' life and ministry). The writing of Mark took place thirty or thirty-five years after Jesus' resurrection. Consequently, you would need to know the period of Jesus' life and ministry and the particular circumstances in the Roman world which produced the writing. You would profit by reading books on Bible history and studying its exciting drama. The more you study your text in the light of the period or periods with which it is connected the better you will understand what the text meant originally.

Placing the passage in its historical setting will lead to various historical facts. You will learn about the human author and his particular situation. The author of a passage had a unique personality and distinctive views. He spoke out of an immediate life situation and out of a distinctive religious, cultural, social, and political background. Understanding the author and his situation helps to discover significant factors about the text.

As you learn about the author, you will also learn about the original readers of the book. You will learn about their background, their character, and the environment which determined the ideas, terminology, and manner in which the author addressed them. Knowing both the author and the readers leads naturally to reconstructing the occasion and purpose of the writing. No book in the Bible came from a vacuum. A particular situation called forth the book. The author had a reason for writing. When you reconstruct, as closely as possible, the author and readers along with the occasion and purpose of writing, you stand at a vantage point of understanding the original meaning of the text.

An understanding of the biblical world. As you study different periods of Bible history, various facets of the biblical world will emerge. Geographical, political, economic, and social factors will be reflected in the passage. When you are aware of geographical facts, the message in a text becomes more real. You will need to know that the land of Palestine occupied a prominent place in the Bible. The plains, the deserts, the Mediterranean Sea, the Jordan River, the Sea of Galilee, the Dead Sea, the hills and the mountains make up Palestine. In addition to geographical information about Palestine, you will need to understand something about the neighboring areas of Egypt, Syria, Assyria, Babylon, Asia Minor, Greece, and Italy.

In both the Old and New Testaments political rulers and leaders played an important role in the lives of Jewish people and early Christians. Whenever a ruler or leader is mentioned, you should seek all the information you can get. Knowing the nature of the political circumstances surrounding a text would be of great help in interpreting the meaning of the writing.

When you look at the historical scene in which the message of God came, you will also observe economic conditions. The matters of trade, agriculture, craftsmen and their products, and travel by sea and land helped determine the economy. You will notice that natural calamities such as floods, droughts, and earthquakes affected economic conditions. Without some understanding of the economic conditions, you cannot enter fully into a message which came to a particular people in a particular situation.

As you study the Bible for a sermon, you will need to be aware of social-religious situations. The word of the Lord came to a people with customs different from the Western world. The Israelites observed special ceremonies in the birth of their children and in their marriages. Legal transactions took place at the gate of the city. Religious life found expression in the tabernacle, in the Temple, in the synagogue, and in the local congregations of Christians. Most of the people of the biblical world lived in the cities and worked outside the cities in the fields. The social structures—slave and free persons, the rich and the poor—made ancient society quite different from the kind of society we know in the West. Before the situation can be interpreted correctly, the social and religious customs need to be understood.

To study Bible history and to learn various facts about the biblical world, you need to get some basic books. You would profit by careful study of Bible histories, of Bible atlases, and of Bible encyclopedias or dictionaries. Also, most reputable commentaries will contain a small amount of the history surrounding the text, as well as insights into geographical, political, economic, social, and religious conditions.

An example of background material. Studying the text from the historical perspective is not just an academic exercise. It is an attempt to gain understanding of what the text *meant* so you may share with people what the text *means* to their lives. To preach intelligently and therapeutically on a text, you need to be familiar with certain relevant facts which lie largely outside the passage. Most of these historical findings will not be stated explicitly in the sermon. However, the background information will give you an assured grasp of the passage. At times the historical findings will flash through the sermon.

Studying the Bible for a sermon begins with background material. This study includes the following seven matters: Author and/or speakers, person or persons addressed, time, place, occasion, aim, and prominent teaching of the text. As you work with your text from these angles, you will move toward a genuine understanding of the original meaning. You can proceed to help people with the application of the truths of the text. We shall not discuss these seven background matters in detail. Instead we shall provide an example. As you study the examples, you will notice the principles involved in studying a text from its historical perspective.

Background Material on James 1:19-27

1. Author and/or Speaker

    In light of studies in several commentaries, my conclusion is that James, the half-brother of Jesus, was the author of the letter. James was converted after the Lord's resurrection. He became a leader of the church in Jerusalem.[1]

2. Persons Addressed

    The salutation designates the readers as "the

twelve tribes of the dispersion." Three views: (a) All
Jews outside Palestine, (b) Figure language for
Christians in general under symbol of ancient Israel,
(c) Jewish Christians outside Palestine. The letter
seems to be addressed to Jewish Christians. Because
their background is Jewish, they would have listened naturally to a Jewish Christian leader who
resided in Jerusalem. (Hiebert, *Epistle of James,*
(pp. 36-39).[2]

3. Time

The date of James would be determined by your
view of authorship. If you accept the traditional
view, you would place the time of writing from AD
50-60. James was martyred in AD 62. If you accept
another authorship, the date could range from the
end of the first century to the middle of the second
century. More than likely, the early date in James
the Lord's brother's life was the time of writing (AD
50).

4. Place

Acceptance of the traditional view of authorship
carries with it the conclusion that the letter was
written from Jerusalem. This was James' fixed place
of residence. This accords with the references to "the
early and latter rain" (5:7); "a burning heat" (1:11);
"sweet water and bitter" (3:11); the cultivation of
figs and olives, and the imagery of the nearby seas
(1:6; 3:4). All these conditions were reminiscent of
conditions in Palestine.

5. Occasion

There is nothing in the letter to indicate the occasion which brought it forth. James did not indicate a
specific crisis. Perhaps the occasion of Jewish Christians, who were scattered throughout Asia Minor,
prompted the writing. They needed to know how to
apply their faith in Christ.

6. Aim
      The aim of the letter of James was to urge Jewish
    Christians to apply their faith to life.
7. Prominent Teaching of the Text
      The text, James 1:19-27, fits into the overall
    theme of the letter. The central teaching of 1:19-27 is
    "hearing and doing the Word of God."

Other ideas emerge as you study the text carefully,
such as: the role of God's Word, the bridled tongue, the
compassion for the helpless, genuine worship, and moral
purity.

You will notice that the preparation of background
material helps to acquaint you with facts behind the
text. Preparing background material on James 1:19-27
would suffice for other texts in James. Once you do the
background material for a book in the Bible you will be
prepared to put any text for the book in the historical
perspective. Some helpful hints would be beneficial for
you to know as you prepare background material for
your text: (1) Write briefly on seven facts. You do not
need to write more than two pages on all seven points.
Each fact could be an involved discussion, but you are
trying to write brief conclusions of your study. Make
your answers terse, to the point. (2) As you read facts
which lie largely outside the text, think of the matters
which might be helpful for a sermon. (3) Use two or
three commentaries to gather the factual material. Try
not to use too many commentaries at first. This process
is not just a Bible study. It is a study of the text for a
sermon. Along with Bible references, give abbreviations
of sources used and page numbers.

The Analytical Perspective

After studying the text from the historical perspective, you will need to investigate it from the analytical

perspective. This involves knowing the *what, why,* and
how of textual analysis. Before we seek an answer to
these questions, a word needs to be said about the
length of a text.

Your text for a sermon may vary from a part of a
verse to several chapters of a Bible book. Irrespective of
how short your text is, you will analyze the verses both
before and after the text. For example, you might select
James 1:22 as a text for a sermon, but you want to know
the context of this verse. So, you would want to investigate James 1:19-27. If you know the flow of thought
leading to a text, and the flow of thought away from it,
you can know with some certainty the flow of thought
within the text itself.

An understanding of textual analysis. Having understood that the length of your text may vary, we can seek
to understand what a textual analysis is. To analyze a
text means to resolve a passage into its parts. It is the
art of discovering the thoughts of a biblical writer. It
comes after diligent reading and careful studying of the
text. It is a work sheet which seeks to present an outline
of a passage. It will disclose clearly the structure and
progression of thought in a passage.

Why should you prepare a textual analysis? The
answer is that you want to catch the flow of a passage so
that you may know the context of each verse, as well as
the meaning of the entire passage. The purpose of a
textual analysis is not to get a sermon outline. Instead,
you analyze a text in order to know what the text *meant*
when it was written so that you may share what it
means now to people in their needs.

How do you do a textual analysis? Four helpful hints
will be given on the procedures of analyzing a passage.
(1) Read and reread the passage from as many translations as you have available. This will be of great help in
interpreting the passage. Of course you would profit
from a study of the text in its original language.

G. Campbell Morgan, the great expository preacher of London in the 1900s, read a text at least fifty times before he sought to build a sermon from it. No other procedures can substitute for the prayerful and careful reading of the text. As you read, seek to discover the main theme of the passage, as well as the secondary subjects and themes.

(2) Divide the text into paragraphs. Give careful consideration to the paragraph divisions in the Revised Standard Version, *The New English Bible,* American Standard Version of 1901, and *The Bible: A New Translation* (Moffatt). You will be especially helped by the paragraph titles in *The New English Bible* and in *The New International Version.* For example, *The New International Version* divides James 1:19-27 into three sections under the general title "Listening and Doing" (1:19-21,22-25,26-27).

(3) State the principle idea of each paragraph. Mark those paragraphs either with Arabic (1,2,3,4) or Roman numerals (I,II,III,IV). This procedure will get you to the main points of the textual analysis. You will understand the main flow of the passage with the paragraphs.

(4) Read and study each paragraph again to discover subordinate or contributing ideas which amplify, sustain, or elaborate upon the principle idea. Use some type of numbering (1,2,3,4) or lettering (a, b, c, d) to designate these subservient ideas.

An example of textual analysis. Studying a text from the analytical perspective is not a luxury. Doing this kind of analysis will help you get your sermon. Through the textual analysis, you seek to understand the flow of the text. An example of a textual analysis follows.

Analysis of James 1:19-27

I.   The hearing of God's Word. 1:19-20
    A.   The eagerness to listen. 1:19
    B.   The reason for listening. 1:20

II.   The reception of God's Word. 1:21
    A.   The reception of God's Word with openness. 1:21*a*
    B.   The prerequisite to receiving God's Word. 1:21*b*
    C.   The manner of receiving God's Word. 1:21*c*
    D.   The motivation for receiving God's Word. 1:21*d*
III.   The obedience to God's Word. 1:22-27
    A.   The command to obedience. 1:22
    B.   The illustration of obedience. 1:23-25
    C.   The application of acceptable obedience. 1:26-27

You will notice that analyzing the text helps you understand it thoroughly. You catch something of a flow which came from the inspired author. The analysis of a passage is a helpful exercise which aids your understanding of a text and provides a process of moving smoothly to sermon preparation.

The Exegetical Perspective

Having examined your text from both the historical and analytical perspective, you will be ready to study it from the exegetical perspective. To study a text from the exegetical perspective means to examine different grammatical factors. You will need to study your text in-depth, and this exercise provides this opportunity.

An understanding of biblical literature. One of the first matters to consider exegetically about your text is its type of literature. The Bible has all kinds of literature: historical narration, poetry, parables, sermons, conversation, apocalyptic, symbols, allegories, similitudes, figures of speech, and other literary types. Many books of the Old Testament utilize historical narration. The book of Psalms is a collection of 150 hymns or Jewish poetry. Most of the writings of Paul followed the basic form of first-century letter writing.

You will need to look closely at your text and determine its literary type. Is it historical narration? Is it prose or poetry? Is the language literal or figurative? Different kinds of language are interpreted differently. Interpreting Jewish poetry as prose opens the door for all kinds of misunderstanding. You could misunderstand a passage by interpreting a literal passage as figurative or a figurative passage as literal. Determine to the best of your ability the type of biblical literature which your text is.

An understanding of biblical language. The Bible was written in human languages. You need to look closely at the various factors of the biblical language or you might miss the real meaning of the passage. To study the biblical language means a close examination of words and their meanings. You may obtain this kind of information from Bible dictionaries, commentaries, and specialists in word studies. Different translations and paraphrases of Scripture will also be helpful with word meanings.

You can study a biblical word from its etymology or the root from which the word was derived. Also, you can study a biblical word by examining its usages in other texts. Attention should be given to comparative passages which have the same word. A concordance would be helpful for this type of study.

Another point to consider in the study of the biblical language is the grammatical relationships of words. Words mean what they mean as they stand in relation to each other. You need to study words in their relationships. Good translations and commentaries help with the delicate meanings of verbs, nouns, clauses, adjectives, adverbs, and their relationships.

Closely akin to the study of the biblical language are the various means of expressions which the biblical writers used. The people of the Bible land expressed themselves differently than American people do. You cannot force their expressions into the exactness of modern, Western thought and logic. For example, the expression, "I loved Jacob, and I hated Esau" (Mal. 1:2-3) is a unique Hebrew expression. It is not an opposite as much as it is a comparison. The meaning seemed to have been a comparison of God's love being greater for Jacob.

The examination of biblical literature and biblical language involves a close-up look into a text. You will have moved from the general historical and analytical matter to the detailed and specific factors in the text. To understand the meaning of a text so that you may build sermons to meet people's needs, not one of the three perspectives can be neglected.

An example of exegetical work. When you understand some sound principles of grammatical study, you can proceed with exegetical work. We want to give you some practical, helpful hints in doing exegetical work. (1) Use your analysis of a text as the broad outline for your exegesis. In other words, fit your word study in relationship to the analysis. (2) Record references to commentaries and to Scripture. (3) Try to be as brief and understandable as possible with your exegetical work. (4) Give careful consideration to prominent words and phrases. (5) Examine grammatical relationships of verbs, nouns, adjectives, and clauses.

Perhaps one way to learn how to do an exegesis of a text is to observe the following example. This example will furnish simple exegetical work on a portion of James 1:19-27. Exegetical work may be longer and more involved than the background and the analysis.

Exegetical Work on James 1:19-27
I.   *The hearing of God's Word.* 1:19-20
        A.   *The eagerness to listen.* 1:19
                Verse 19: "Swift to hear, slow to speak, slow to wrath." These words suggest an eagerness

to listen to God's Word. These words call for
careful listening. They warn against quick
speaking and against resentful feelings.
Anger is a hindrance to hearing of God's
Word.

B. *The reason for listening.* 1:20

Verse 20: "Wrath of man." Man's wrath hinders the attaining of righteousness and accom-
plishing the duty which God's Word enjoins.
"Righteousness of God"—could mean "being
right with God" and "doing right." Most biblical writers could not conceive of a person who
was right with God, who did not from the
right relationship begin to do what was right
in relation to God and to other people. (Mit-
ton, *Ep. of J.,* p. 62).

II. *The reception of God's Word.* 1:21

A. *The reception of God's Word with openness.*
1:21*b*

Verse 21: "Receive"—the word suggests duty.
It was used in Acts 17:11 to refer to the reception of the Bereans to God's Word. To *receive*
means to open your life to the powerful influence of God's Word. "Engrafted Word"—J. B.
Mayor interprets the adjective "engrafted" to
mean "rooted" (Mayor, *Ep. of J.,* p. 68). It
means God's Word is rooted.

B. *The prerequisite to receiving God's Word.*
1:21*a*

Verse 21*a*: "Lay apart"—This means to dis-
card. The tense of the Greek verb suggests a
single and decisive act. The figure is that of
stripping and casting aside a dirty garment.
"Filthiness" denotes all that is impure in God's
sight. "Naughtiness" is a specific word which
means a disposition bent on doing harm to
others. "Superfluity" means an abundance.

C.   *The manner of receiving God's Word.* 1:21*c*
Verse 21*c*: "With meekness"—Meekness means the opposite of a self-assertive spirit. It is a teachable spirit.

D.   *The motivation for receiving God's Word.* 1:21*d*
Verse 21*d*: "Save your souls"—The Word of God properly received will promote holiness and develop character.

Bibliography

[1]Hiebert, Edmond D., *The Epistle of James: Tests of a Living Faith* (Chicago: Moody Press, 1979).

[2]Mayor, J. B. *The Epistle of St. James* (Grand Rapids: Baker Book House, 1954).

[3]Mitton, C. Leslie. *The Epistle of James* (Grand Rapids: William B. Eerdmans Publishing Company, 1966).

[4]Songer, Harold S. "James" Vol. XII of *The Broadman Bible Commentary,* ed. by Clifton J. Allen, 12 vols. (Nashville: Broadman Press, 1972).

[5]Vaughan, Curtis. *James: A Study Guide* (Grand Rapids: Zondervan Publishing House, 1969).

Studying the Bible for a sermon is no easy task. However, you must study what the text *meant* so that you can share what it *means.* Heinrich Ott, a German theologian, once said that preaching has two poles—a *then* and a *now.* He also said that a preacher's task in a sermon was to make "a hermeneutical arch" from the then to the now. If you start with the then, you must move to the now. If you begin with the now, you must move to the then. Staying with the *then* of James 1:19-27 would only be a Bible lesson. Dealing with the *now* of listening would be removed from the authoritative foundation of God's Word. When the then and now are combined, you have a Bible truth (then) which can be used to meet people's needs (now). Study carefully a text from the historical, analytical, and exegetical perspectives. These exercises will get you to biblical truth. You will then proceed to relate these biblical truths to the needs of people.

Notes

1. If you were preparing background material of Mark 2:1-12, you would need to consider both author and speakers. For example, you would need to know about John Mark as the author. You would also need to study the speakers in the text. Mark wrote 2:1-5. Then Jesus spoke (cf. 2:5). After Jesus spoke, the scribes spoke (cf. 2:7). Then Jesus spoke again (cf. 2:8-11). The crowd spoke (cf. 2:12).

2. When you draw from a source, identify the source by abbreviations. Give the author's last name, abbreviate the title, and designate the page number. For example, (Hiebert, *Ep. of J.*, pp. 36-39).

3
Putting People in Sermons

Consciously or subconsciously most people listen to sermons in order to be helped. They come with the same question that an ancient king secretly put to a prophet in a time of difficulty: "Is there any word from the Lord?" (Jer. 37:17). Is there any fresh word from God to help solve or live with the various problems of life? People do not attend worship to hear essays or words of general address. In the complicated times of the twentieth century, people desperately yearn to hear a word from God which will give them a reason as well as a resource for living.

God intended sermons for people. The unique idea of proclaiming the Word of God started with the idea of helping people. The earliest forms of proclamation started centuries before Christ with the prophets, scribes, and other Old Testament leaders. The act of preaching reached its highest point when "Jesus came into Galilee, preaching the gospel of the kingdom of God" (Mark 1:14). The finest example of messages helping people can be seen in the ministry of Jesus. The Lord confronted people in the commonplace situations and presented great truths so people could be helped. When Jesus preached, people had burdens lifted. They felt a closeness with God that gave life meaning. They gained courage to face their weaknesses. They saw their failures not with fatalistic pessimism but with new possibilities. They found therapy in Jesus to resolve their selfishness manifested in hatred, prejudice, pride, and sensualism When Jesus preached, people were allowed the possibilities of growth. Jesus helped people in his proclamation mainly because he put people in his messages. His sermons were delivered as a means to help people.

A major exphasis needs to be placed on preparing and delivering sermons so the listener can benefit from the message. All preaching should have for its main business the direct constructive meeting of some problem which puzzles the mind, burdens the conscience, or distracts life. People have a tendency to listen to what is being said when the sermon touches where they live. Facts, events, principles, outlines, and stories become interesting and important when they relate and offer means of help to the hearer.

You can also put people in the sermon by attempting to prepare and to deliver a sermon *with* people not *before* them. Building a sermon does not consist of constructing a sermon which you merely show to others. Instead, sermons are constructed with the idea of being with people. Seeking to put people in preaching will involve preaching from a person, preaching to people's needs, and preaching with people.

Preaching from a Person

You first begin to put people in sermons when you acknowledge and confess your own personhood. Sermons originate from a person. You are a person addressing other people. You are not an expert in Christianity, informing interested hearers; you are a person sharing some of your most intimate and profound personal experiences with other persons. People-centered sermons begin with a prepared person, not just a prepared sermon.

The introspection of the preacher. Acknowledging and confessing your humanness goes a long way in building sermons to meet people's needs. As you examine yourself, you will discover numerous life situations. Discovering these life situations will furnish abundant ideas for sermons. Of course this does not mean that you will parade strengths, weaknesses, and areas of improvement before your audience. Self-examination for the preacher will enable you to say: "I am a human being. Other people must be struggling with these same problems. I must preach on these problems."

Listen to your own spirit and feelings. As you hear the needs of your life, you can be assured that you will hear the pressing needs of those who listen to you. Others, too, struggle with the same kind of problems and situations. Self-examination can be an agony and an ecstasy. We want to share some of the ideas from our lives which have produced sermons:

—How can I be related properly to God?
—How may I be a better Christian?
—How can I develop and maintain a healthy self-image?
—How can I get along with people?
—How will this disappointment affect me?
—How do I deal with my fears and anxieties?
—How do I face this crisis in my life?
—How can the pain of grief be eased?
—How can I adjust to this stage of life through which I am passing?
—How can I face death realistically?

If we struggle with these and other problems, other human beings may be struggling with the same problems. This means that sermon subjects often arise from monitoring the tremors of personal experiences. Hearing the needs of your own life will lead to seeking for a word from God for that need. As you discover God's therapy for your personal situation, you are in a better position to use these situations as subject material for sermons.

Confessional preaching is the way you began to preach. Having found forgiveness for sin through faith in Jesus Christ, you told others in your sermons, "Believe on the Lord Jesus Christ." A need had been met in your life, and you went to others to confess and to share the answer for this same need. The pilgrimage with Christ is shared as you move through life. If you are going to put people in your sermons, you must first of all put yourself in your sermons. This takes acknowledgment and ownership of your needs.

The preacher's observation of life. Sermons originate from the preacher's observation of life about him. Building sermons to help people will involve sending out your listening antenna in every conceivable direction. You can put people into sermons by listening carefully to life as it takes place around you. Authentic preaching will need to take on a situational dimension. These historical situations present exciting possibilities for listening to people.

Life is not dull. It is not without its interesting events. Some historical events from which sermon ideas could come are:
— The assassination of a president or other outstanding leader
   The international incidents
— The occurrence of moral scandals
— The death of a great person
— The economic conditions—inflation or recession
— Tragedies of enormous magnitude

You can interest people when you deal with various national, international, or local situations. Reading news analyses helps you to orient sermons toward conditions in which your people live. These episodes consume the thoughts of people.

Some examples might be helpful. Economic conditions such as a serious recession could call forth a sermon of Jesus' view of material possessions. Or, the death of some world leader could motivate a message about facing death or coping with grief.

Develop a sensitivity to life as it moves on about you. As you hear the news and the analyses of the news, listen to life. This is where people are.

The visitation of the preacher. The preacher can enhance sermon preparation and delivery by pastoral visitation. Harry Emerson Fosdick is recognized as an outstanding preacher of the twentieth century. He emphasized the close relationship between pastoral care and preaching. As he talked and shared life with his parishioners, many subjects for his sermons arose. Speaking about the secret of Fosdick's effective preaching, John D. Rockefeller, Jr. is reported to have said, "The greatness of his preaching lies in the fact that each person in the congregation thinks he is preaching to him. I never hear him but I say, 'How does he know my problem?' "[1]

Pastoral calling cannot be viewed as an appendix to the ministry. Through visitation you learn about the specific needs of the people. Through visitation you gather ideas for preaching. Phillips Brooks said, "The preacher needs to be a pastor, that he may preach to real men. The pastor must be preacher, that he may keep the dignity of his work alive. The preacher, who is not a pastor, grows remote. The pastor, who is not a preacher grows petty . . . . Be both; for you cannot really be one unless you also are the other."[2]

Through pastoral calling, the preacher gains valuable insights into the lives of people. He learns their troubles, their hopes and aspiration, their religious orientation, and their particular life situations. As you share indepth with the lives of the people, you can then speak with perception to a particular congregation. The awesome power of listening to people motivates the flowing of sermon ideas.

    —Why am I suffering?

—How can I get out of guilt?
—Does it make a difference how I live?
—Why does my loved one suffer?
—Can I master this fear?
—Does God know that I exist?
—Was it God's will for that young father to die?

Hearing these needs from pastoral calling motivates the preacher to construct a sermon to that particular need. Contact with people tends to put people in the sermon.

Preaching to People's Needs

Sermons will be people oriented when you think about the various needs of the people. Various needs exist within a community, and God has selected preachers to give them a word from God in these particular situations. Michael Griffiths in his book, *Cinderella with Amnesia,* quotes statistics to show that around the average city church there are 2,000 houses with 10,000 people. You can reckon that from these 2,000 houses there are: 500 households needing a neighborly hand of friendship; 20 unmarried mothers; 100 elderly people living alone; 10 discharged prisoners; 100 deprived children; 10 homeless; 100 broken marriages; 20 families in debt; 100 juvenile delinquents who have been before the courts in the last three years, 80 persons in the hospital; 80 alcoholics."[3]

Edgar N. Jackson, in his book *How to Preach to People's Needs,* gave valuable insight about needs present in a typical congregation. In a church of five hundred people, it is reasonable to assume that at least one hundred have been so recently bereaved as to feel an acute sense of loss. Probably a third of the married persons face problems of personality adjustment that may weaken or destroy their homelife. At least half of the five hundred can be assumed to have problems of emotional adjustment to school, work, home, or community that endanger their happiness. Others may have neuroses ranging from alcohol addiction to lesser forms of obsessions and anxiety states. Perhaps fifteen or more may be homosexually inclined and another twenty-five depressed. Another hundred may suffer from feelings of guilt so that their peace of mind and health are jeopardized. Seeing this picture of people heightens your sense of building and delivering sermons to meet human needs.

The awareness of human needs. You need an understanding of basic human needs if you are to build sermons. One who builds sermons needs an elementary understanding of human behavior. Human beings are physical organisms and psychological creatures. Scholars assert that the basic needs of every person are love, belonging, attention, appreciation, discipline, sex, and God. The famous psychologist Abraham Maslow divided human need into seven different categories. His theory of personality would help the preacher to understand the needs of people.

The basic set of needs which motivate people is what Maslow called physiological needs. This is the need for food, oxygen, water, rest, sex, and elimination.

As one's physical needs are met, a new cluster of dominant needs will call for attention. Maslow called these safety needs. These include need for physical shelter, economic security, and emotional stability.

When safety requirements have been met, then the need for love, affection, and the sense of belonging become the focus of one's life. When a person has physical needs satisfied and feels safe in the world, he then wants to relate to other people in a different way. He wants to be loved and have feelings of acceptance.

The next cluster of needs is known as esteem needs. In such needs, human beings search for self-respect, status, recognition, and approval.

After the esteem needs have been met, Maslow then states that human beings long for self-actualization needs. These needs include desire for creativity, mature relationships, deep religious expressions, and feelings of growth. This is a person developing true potential. Self-actualization needs prompt a person to seek wholeness, meaning, and a feeling of autonomy.

As one develops his potential, a new group of motivating needs surface. These cluster around the desire to know and understand. Many people are motivated to know and to understand various factors about life. Finally, Maslow described the top level as aesthetic needs. Such a person has a longing for beauty, order, and harmony.

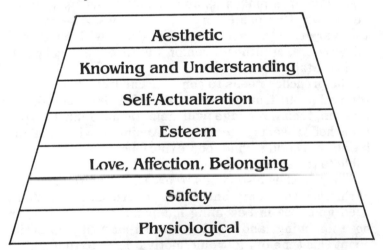

Aesthetic

Knowing and Understanding

Self-Actualization

Esteem

Love, Affection, Belonging

Safety

Physiological

The basic needs of human beings have to be met. Understanding Abraham Maslow's concept of the "hierarchy of needs" will increase your knowledge of human need. His theory helps you understand better the needs of people. Until these basic needs are met in a reliable, continuing manner, a person's life will be dominated by them. He will not be interested deeply in other things while this domination lasts. When the first cluster of needs have been dependably met, Maslow believes that a new and higher set of dominating requirements will take over the motivating center of one's life. The diagram (p. 45) is a model of Maslow's hierarchy of needs.

The understanding of human stages. You will build sermons for various age groups. Few preachers speak Sunday after Sunday to one age group. Within the various age groups, there exist preschool children, school-age children, adolescents, young adults, middle adults, retired adults, and senior adults. Each stage of life presents a challenge for the preacher. Understanding the characteristics of the various stages of life will help you meet human needs in your sermons. Gail Sheehy in the book *Passages* makes us aware of the various stages of adulthood. One pastor preached a series of sermons on the various stages of life. He dealt with childhood, adolescence, adulthood, senior adulthood, and called the series "Stages."

The preacher needs to consider children. They can listen and profit from sermons. Relating the Bible to their lives in their language will help them. John Claypool preached a sermon entitled "Anointed with Delight" based on David's childhood experiences. He related the Bible to the experiences of childhood.

The preacher also needs to preach to youth. The ages of thirteen to twenty-one represent crucial years. Youth need guidance in becoming independent, finding a purpose for living, and moving toward maturity. Learning about this time of life would motivate you to find biblical material relating to these strategic areas.

Most of the audience will be adults. However, the pastor might want to consider the different levels of adults: single, young married adults, married adults with small children, middle-age adults, retired persons, and senior adults. Each age group has various needs which the preacher can deal with through his sermons.

The discerning of personal problems. Every normal person is the victim of attacks of various personal problems. These problems affect the triad of one's being—the mind, body, and emotions. Think about the personal problem of excessive anxiety. Pressures exist in one's external world which make one tense. These pressures come from financial distress, broken relationships, pressing deadlines, and hundreds of other factors. Other people have anxiety without reason. Those who preach must be aware of the anxieties that exist among the people.

Another personal problem discernible in the lives of people is fear. Deep within a person lie the fears of life, of health, and of death. During life's experiences, people develop fearful reactions to situations, objects, and events. You have a great opportunity to preach therapeutic sermons which seek to urge people to face their fears and to trust the Lord.

Students of human nature detect a large percentage of people who suffer from some form of depression. This depression ranges in intensity from mild, short-lived neurosis to chronic, psychotic depression that requires professional care. You have an excellent opportunity to build and to preach sermons from the Bible which deal directly with depression.

Many people come to worship with a load of guilt. Sometimes guilt is the result of sin. You can proclaim God's forgiveness to people with this burden.

Numerous other personal problems could be studied to aid the preacher in his preaching to people's needs. Some other personal problems are as follows: insecurity, loneliness, defeat, doubt, inferiority, injurious habits, and numerous other problems.

The helping with life's crises. Within every audience there are people who suffer from various crises. The crucial times of change in a person's life call forth some sermons which deal with the particular need. Many people in the congregation deal with death in one way or another. Surveys indicate that people, young and old, ask more questions about death and the life beyond than any other subject of a religious nature. Also, many people within a congregation have recently experienced the bereavement of a relative or close friend. The preacher who builds sermons from the Bible on the subject of death or grief can expect a hearing.

Crises come to life when important decisions have to be made. The discerning preacher will recognize that many within the audience struggle with momentous decisions: choosing a vocation, choosing a mate, changing jobs, whether to allow the surgeon to operate, putting a loved one in a nursing home, and hundreds of other decisions. These crises and others demand that sermons be prepared to help people in their needs.

The support for life's relationships. God did not make human beings for isolation. The Lord put man and woman in the world to live together. The Lord gave children to parents. He put different nations at different places. The Lord intended that individuals live together harmoniously.

Human beings have struggled and continue to struggle for healthy human relationships. Only a casual look at the world, the community, the city, and the home discloses fractured relationships. Within every audience every listener struggles with human relationships: children to parents, parents to children, boss to employee, employee to boss, neighbor to neighbor, and in other relationships where one encounters another person or persons.

You can build sermons to enhance human relationships. Abundant texts in both the Old Testament and the New Testament deal with human relationships. Some sermons will need to be constructed to help heal fractured relationships. This is especially true in the area of family problems. Divorcees, alienated youth, and other family difficulties cry out for therapy to cope with the conflict. The preacher occupies a prominent role in offering support for life's relationships.

These areas of preaching to persons have not been exhaustive, definitive, or conclusive. They have been suggestive. You will want to go to the Scriptures and have a word from God for your people.

Preaching with Persons

Building sermons is not constructing something in isolation from people. Of course you will retreat to do the work of research and writing. Sermons can be in the process of construction as you associate with people. To build an authentic sermon you need to be with people.

You have heard church members say about a preacher's sermon, "He wasn't with it today." What did they mean? The key to this kind of remark is in the preposition *with*. The word describes a close connection or an intimate association. If the preacher wants to be "with it," he needs to consider seriously the art of connecting his personhood, his text, and his sermons with the people.

The connection of the preacher with the audience. Preaching involves the sharing of one's self with other people. Phillips Brooks' classic definition of preaching as communication of God's truth through human personality suggests how the preacher connects with the audience. He connects with an audience by being himself. He does not have to put on a ministerial front. He begins to be "with the audience" when he is himself with God's Word. The congregation is more capable of experiencing God's truth when they are in the process of experiencing the understanding of the person who seeks to preach God's Word.

Moreover, the preacher who wants to be "with it" needs to be an empathizing person. The preacher will want to be able to perceive, sense, feel, and understand the audience. When the preacher understands the people to whom he preaches, he can choose the words and

the forms of presentation that they understand. The
audience then experiences understanding. Edgar N.
Jackson said:

> The capacity for sensitivity, the ability to feel with
> and for his people, is a pastor's supreme art . . .
> The preacher who is able to move into the thought
> and feeling of his people, who is able to achieve
> identity with them creates the mood for effective
> interchange. In any relationship where there is no
> chance to talk back, a special atmosphere can be
> created wherein persons can *feel* back.[4]

Building sermons to meet people's needs requires building of the preacher. The capacity to empathize with
others does not happen accidently. It takes preparation
of the person to hear, to feel, and to see the congregation.

The connection of the text with the audience. The
preacher is "with it" when in his sermons the Bible connects with twentieth-century living. Sermons cannot be
separated from biblical revelation. Otherwise, it would
not be Christian preaching. The preacher is inseparably
bound to the Bible. Paul said, "For we preach not ourselves, but Christ Jesus the Lord; and ourselves your
servants for Jesus' sake" (2 Cor. 4:5). The preacher
cannot escape the task of understanding the basic message of the Bible. He will need to understand as much as
possible about life situations from the text. Preaching
can never be separated from biblical revelation.

You could possibly know about Bible times and not
associate ancient situation with contemporary situations. Having drawn the picture of the biblical situation,
you will need to bring it home in concrete illustrations.
To be "with it," the preacher must connect the biblical
then with contemporary now. Preachers are "with it"
when they are with the meaning of the text. They are
also "with it" when the text relates to human situations

in today's world. When the biblical truth touches the living situation, sermons happen which meet people's needs.

The connection of sermon form with the audience. You are "with it" when some type of order is used to present the biblical truth for people's needs. Structuring a sermon is an art to facilitate communication. Two extremes exist with regard to form. On one hand, some build a sermon with the sole emphasis on structure. On the other hand, others so reject structure and advocate freedom from structure that they have formlessness. The form presented in this book is one which studies the Bible seriously, looks at the needs of people closely, and then puts the sermon in a proposition. The proposition is then developed in order to achieve the sermon's stated objective in the lives of those who hear.

Do you want to be "with it" when you preach? First, be the person God has made and is making you. Second, study your text carefully and connect it to your people. Third, take the audience seriously. Fourth, use the structure to facilitate communication.

Notes

1. James W. Clarke, *Dynamic Preaching* (Westwood, New Jersey: Fleming H. Revell Company, 1960), p. 68.

2. Phillips Brooks, *Lectures on Preaching* (London: H. R. Allenson, 1902), p. 77.

3. Michael C. Griffiths, *Cinderella with Amnesia* (Downers Grove, Illinois: InterVarsity Press, 1975), pp. 170-171.

4. Edgar N. Jackson, *A Psychology for Preaching* (Manhasset, New York: Channel Press, 1961), p. 64.

4
Focusing on One Sermon Idea

Where do you start in the building of a sermon? The beginning point for a sermon is an idea from the Bible for the needs of people. The sermon idea may be premature and undeveloped when first conceived, but it is the place where you start in building the sermon. Where do you get the idea? The conception of a sermon idea may occur almost any place—studying the Bible, reading a book, studying a Bible commentary, driving a car, watching television, talking with another person, or numerous other experiences. You cannot predict where a sermon idea will be born.

No easy answers may be given to improve the birth of sermon ideas. Determining fresh, new ideas week after week is one of the hardest struggles of the pastor. Nothing will substitute for a disciplined life. This will mean consistent, laborious study of the Bible, stewardship of work habits, a devotional life, and an openness for personal growth and learning.

Now we want to begin the process of building a sermon. We shall start with focusing upon one idea for a sermon. In this chapter we shall discuss the relationship of sermon idea and text, the anatomy of a sermon idea, the essence of the text, and the essence of the sermon.

The Relationship of Sermon Idea and Text

Studying the Bible and listening for people's needs will provide more than adequate sermon ideas and content. You will need to study the Bible carefully. You will also need intellectual and experiential knowledge of people and their needs. In other words, you will need to learn both the Bible and the congregation.

From the Bible to idea. You will need to keep the reading and studying of the Bible uppermost in your ministry. The Bible will serve as the catalyst for sermon ideas. How do you use the Bible for sermon ideas? First, read the Bible from many translations. New translations offer a freshness from the one you read consistently. Vary your reading in the Bible. You need to read from the Old Testament and from the New Testament. Do not fail to read even the less read books of the Bible such as Leviticus, 1 and 2 Chronicles, Revelation, and others. If possible, read and study the Bible from the original languages.

Second, think about what you have read from the Bible. Do some creative brooding over your Bible readings. Think about what the truths you read say to you. Allow provocative words, phrases, or stories, to speak to you.

Third, listen to the Bible. Try, as closely as possible, to overhear what the biblical writers said. The Lord will speak to you through the written record of his Word. Others have heard God speak from the Bible. You can hear him speak to you too.

From your dynamic involvement with the Bible, sermon ideas will emerge. One pastor affirmed that he studied the Bible four hours each day for five days each week. His systematic Bible study not only produced next Sunday's sermon but sermon ideas for months or even years ahead.

From idea to the Bible. You will also need to keep the needs of people uppermost in your mind. People with their diverse needs will serve as a source for sermon ideas. How do you get sermon ideas from your people? Nothing will substitute for personal association and in-

volvement with the people. In order to draw ideas from
the lives of our hearers, you need to have a growing
knowledge and a love for your people. You will discover
numerous sermon ideas when you observe and empathize with the people in their peculiar and particular life
circumstances.

You can also get sermon ideas by reading about people. Read newspapers and magazines about people in the
news. Analyze closely the needs of people through diversified reading in novels, biographies, diaries, journals,
and history. In addition to association with people and
reading about people, observe people in-depth. Watch
how they act; what they like; how they spend their time;
what they buy. Be alert and aware of the life-style of
people about you.

The question always comes, Should the sermon idea
start with the text or with the needs of people? The obvious answer is, Either one! If you start with a text, seek
to relate the textual truth to the needs of your people.
When discovery of a person's need comes first, seek to
find a text which relates to that particular need. The
contemporary experience in Christ and the historic revelation of the Word must always be in dynamic interplay.
Therefore, getting an idea for a sermon requires two
qualities. First, you must listen to the text and seek to
relate it to the needs of people. Second, you must listen
to people and relate these needs to biblical truths.

When delivered, a sermon should disclose biblical
truth and contemporary relevance. To know the Word is
not enough. To know the world is not enough. Preaching
which meets the challenge of the age must seek the con-
frontation of the living God with living people through
the living Word. The preacher must struggle and fight
for this meeting point of world and Word. The preparation of a summary of the text and the process of getting a
proposition will help the Word and the world to meet.

The Anatomy of a Sermon Idea

Every sermon should have one major idea. Everything about the sermon should develop, support, or illustrate one thought. The audience ought to hear only one idea. Even the casual listener should be able to produce the preacher's central thought in one sentence. In this book, all the mechanics will focus on one-idea sermons. Before we proceed to the process of building the sermon, we want to give you a quick overview of a sermon.

An overview of the sermon idea. Looking at the whole of something might help you understand the parts. We would like to give a brief, general overview of our process of building a sermon. In the subsequent chapters, we shall study specific, practical insights related to the following areas: text, essence of the text in a sentence (ETS), proposition (essence of the sermon in a sentence or ESS), objective, probing question, unifying word, transitional sentences, development (outline), substance material, introduction, conclusion, and illustrations. All of these factors will be used in the process of building sermons to meet people's needs.

(1) The text either furnishes or substantiates the idea for the sermon. You could have studied the text, and it inspired the sermon idea; or, you could have observed a person's need, and the need pointed to the text. Either way, the text is vital to the sermon idea.

(2) To start sermon construction, you will want to summarize the message of the text in a simple sentence. The summary may be called *the essence of the text in a sentence* (ETS). Summarizing the text leads naturally to the next stage of the sermon-building process. The ETS will be discussed fully in this chapter.

(3) You will want to have a biblically based and people-oriented sermon *proposition* (ESS). This involves the

statement of the truth of the text related to people's
needs in a simple sentence. The proposition will relate to
the ETS and will furnish the foundation upon which the
rest of the sermon will be built. The proposition is the
sermon in one sentence and is discussed later in this
chapter.

(4) After you prepare the ETS and the ESS, you will
state your *objective* for the sermon. This will be a simple
sentence in which you will state specifically the action
you want your hearers to take as a result of listening to
the message. The objective will be studied in chapter 5.

(5) The means of securing development is through the
use of a *probing question* put to the proposition. The
probing question leads to the selection of a *unifying
word*. The *major divisions* emerge from the proposition
by asking the probing question, and this produces the
unifying word which holds the divisions together. You
will get more information on these matters in chapter 6.

(6) The development needs *substance material*. Each
major division needs to be expanded. Several sentences
furnish expansion for each major division. *Illustrations*
furnish practical examples throughout the sermon of
various facets of ideas. Substance material and illustrations will be discussed fully in chapter 6.

(7) Now let us say a word about introduction, conclusion, and transitional sentences. The *introduction* leads
people to the idea. Generally, a *transitional sentence*
will take people smoothly from the introduction to the
first major division. The *conclusion* leads people from
the idea to action. It shares with people how the idea
relates to their lives, and it persuades them to live the
idea. All of these matters will be studied in chapter 7.

(8) The *topic* may result either before or after the
sermon-building process. It is the name you give to the
sermon.

The naming of the sermon idea—topic. The sermon
begins with an idea. You may think of some form of a

topic as you start your sermon building. However, the phrasing of the topic will not be finalized until the sermon has been completed.

The example of a one-idea sermon. Perhaps one of the best ways to clarify the meaning of the anatomy of an idea is to demonstrate the principles which have been stated briefly. Details of the principles will be presented in subsequent chapters. The following parts of the sermon will furnish an example of a sermon which develops one idea.

Topic: Who Do You Think You Are?

Text: Luke 15:11-24

ETS: The younger son in the parable struggled to find out who he was.

Proposition: We can have a good self-image.

Objective: I want people to accept themselves with a balanced self-image.

Probing Question: What are some possible self-images?

Unifying Word: *Images*

Transitional Sentence: Let us notice some possible *images* we may possess.

I.   We may have an inflated self-image.
   A.   Centering life completely around ourselves causes an overinflated image.
   B.   Depending upon ourselves exaggerates our image.

II.   We may have a deflated self-image.
   A.   Living by our rules in a God-made world degrades us.
   B.   Valuing life by materialistic standards lowers the value of human life.

III.   We may have a balanced self-image.
   A.   Looking honestly at ourselves raises our sense of worth.
   B.   Hearing God's estimation as "son" helps us know that he values us.

Now we need to take the time and effort to learn together how to build a one-idea sermon. We shall work stage by stage, and we shall try to give examples of the principles as we proceed.

The Essence of the Text

Meaningful preaching gives a central place to biblical interpretation. Christians acknowledge the Bible as the normative guide for life. The text of a sermon has a vital connection with the sermon idea. It is not brought in for the sake of being courteous to ancient and revered Scripture. It has a vital connection with the human situation. Whether a sermon starts from a life situation or from a scriptural situation, the two will meet in the beginning of the sermon-building process. As we have said previously, you may start a sermon with a person's need, but you must search for scriptural support. You may start a sermon from study of the Scripture, but you will need to intersect the biblical truth with life today. The process of sermon building begins, then, with awareness of two specific matters: the biblical situation and the needs of people.

Bringing biblical truth and people's needs together will start with the writing of two crucial sentences—the essence of the text (ETS) and the sermon proposition (ESS). The ETS will always be in the past tense, and the ESS will be either in the present or future tense. These two sentences (ETS and ESS) will help the sermon to be based on the Bible and to be related to people's needs. We need to learn first the facts and mechanics about an ETS.

The text studied. Before you can state an ETS, the text must be studied carefully. The sermon proceeds from the Bible and connects with the situations of the hearers. It does not arise from religion in general and address the universe. Understanding the text is a crucial aspect of preparing a sermon. You may ask, How can I

understand this text so that God speaks his message
through me to the needs of people? You will note that in
chapter 2 we shared general principles about studying
the Bible. Using these general principles, we want to
discuss the specific study of a text. The purpose of this
study will be to produce an ETS.

The first specific act in studying the text will be to
hear the text in its original biblical setting. You will hear
what the text meant when it was first written. Learning
about its original setting will require you to relate the
text to the book and to the chapter where it is located.
For example, if Philippians 1:19-26 has been chosen as a
text, or if the idea was discovered elsewhere and you
were led to Philippians 1:19-26, you must understand
the setting of the text. Studying the origin of the letter
of Philippians would be helpful. This would disclose
Paul's affection for the believers in Philippi and his
future plans. Paul awaited the outcome of his Roman
imprisonment. You will understand Philippians 1:19-26
better when you read it in the light of the Philippian letter. In addition to the life situation of Philippians, you
will need to put Philippians 1:19-26 in its immediate context. This seems to be Philippians 1:12-26. In 1:12-18
Paul discussed various situations which arose from his
imprisonment, and in 1:19-26 he discussed the dilemma
regarding his future.

Having oriented the text to its setting and immediate
context, you must proceed to seek information about
grammatical matters. Study the text in its original language if possible. Reading the text in numerous English
translations and paraphrases will yield many insights.
The interpreter will need to understand the particular
literature of the text—whether it is poetry as in the
Psalms, parables as in the Gospels, or historical narration such as the book of Acts. The interpreter will also
examine key words of the text and the usage of these
words in other places in the Bible. For this exercise, you

can consult concordances, Bible dictionaries, commentaries, and books on word studies.

For example, when Philippians 1:19-26 has been oriented to its original setting, you will be sure to secure pertinent grammatical matters from the text. To do this you might write an outline of the large context in order to catch the flow of the passage. An outline of Philippians 1:12-26 is as follows:

1. Paul had unexpected results of his imprisonment. 1:12-14.
   a. The gospel advanced because of Paul's adversities. 1:12.
   b. The whole praetorian guard knew about the gospel. 1:13.
   c. The brethren renewed their confidence with Paul's example. 1:14.
2. Paul had observed Christian workers with their mixed motives. 1:15-18.
   a. Some preach from envy and rivalry. 1:15a, 17.
   b. Others preach from goodwill. 1:15b-16.
   c. Paul rejoiced over the results not the motives. 1:18.
3. Paul expressed his dilemma as well as his confidence in life and death. 1:19-26.
   a. Paul wanted deliverance from prison. 1:19-20.
   b. Paul's view of life and death was in Christ. 1:21.
   c. Paul could live, and it would mean more earthly ministry. 1:22.
   d. Paul might die, and it would mean a greater life with the Lord. 1:23-26.

This outline helps you get the feeling of Paul. Having caught the flow of the passage, you will need to study pertinent words and phrases such as—"furtherance of the gospel," "bonds," "envy and strife," "contention," "life," "death," "gain," "strait betwixt two," "depart," "with Christ," "rejoice." The study of these grammatical factors will enhance your ability to state an ETS.

The text summarized. Having studied your text seriously, you are ready to summarize it. You can never predict just when the right ETS will come to mind. Sometimes it will come readily, even while reading the text for the first time. At other times the ETS will come after long meditation, diligent prayer, and hard study.

The ETS should be a simple sentence which does not exceed fifteen words. It will always be stated in the past tense, for this is an attempt to summarize what the text meant. You have a variety of ways to get an ETS from a text. One way is to state the summary of the text directly from the text. You might even use the words of the text. For example, one ETS of Genesis 5:24 could be: "Enoch walked with God." This is not too hard to summarize, for the words come directly from the text. Another way to state the ETS is from an obvious meaning of the text. For example, an ETS obvious in Matthew 13:1-9 (the parable of four types of soils) would be: "Jesus illustrated how people listened to the gospel."

Also, the ETS could be suggested by the text. This does not mean that the ETS will be less biblical. It means that intensive study of the text leads to a summary contained or inferred. When you connect the text with a subject, you may get an ETS which suggests an idea. A prominent example of the ETS suggested by the text is Luke 15:11-24: "The younger son struggled with his self-image." The idea of self-image is neither directly stated nor immediately obvious. However, as you study Jesus' story, the idea of the young man striving to discover his identity becomes evident. Stating the particular ETS will be influenced by your personal interest or observations and by the particular needs of your people.

The ETS has three primary usages. (1) Studying the text for an ETS grounds the sermon in the biblical situation. (2) You will use the ETS to get a proposition (ESS). (3) In addition to the valuable use of ETS as a guide in preparing the sermon, you will utilize the ETS in the introduction and throughout the body of the sermon. So, getting an ETS is no waste of time. Rather, it is a valuable process in the construction of a sermon.

The examples of ETS. You will need to learn the art of getting an ETS. As you study the Scriptures and observe the needs of your people, you will develop the art of summarizing a text with a sentence telling one facet of what the text meant. We want to furnish five examples of the essence of a text. These same five texts and ETS will be used in the other processes of sermon construction.

(1) **Text:** Genesis 5:24
     ETS: Enoch walked with God.
(2) **Text:** Mark 2:1-12
     ETS: Jesus helped a paralyzed man.
(3) **Text:** Ephesians 2:1-10
     ETS: Paul described Christians as God's workmanship.
(4) **Text:** James 1:19-26
     ETS: James taught believers how to respond to God's Word.
(5) **Text:** Philippians 1:19-26
     ETS: Paul faced the reality of his death.

From our discusssion of the ETS and from the above examples, we want to remind you of the following facts.

(1) The ETS is a simple sentence in the past tense of fifteen words or less.

(2) Each text may have numerous other truths, but you will select one major truth, and you will summarize it.

(3) The ETS results from a careful and diligent study of the text.

(4) The ETS serves as a process of moving you to the proposition and to the other stages of sermon construction.

The Proposition of the Sermon (ESS)

Building a sermon depends upon one clear, biblical idea related to the needs of people. When you state the ETS, you need to work on the proposition. The proposition is the essence of the sermon in a sentence (ESS). It is a simple sentence of not more than fifteen words which should be stated either in the present or in the future tense. Some find the stating of the proposition to be the hardest and most exacting labor in sermon preparation. However, since this is the sermon in a nutshell, it is essential that you work on the proposition until you are satisfied with it. Our contention is that after the text and idea come together in your mind, then the ETS and the ESS will be the starters for sermon construction.

The necessity of a proposition. One of the classical works on sermon preparation is Austin Phelp's book *The Theory of Preaching.* His theory of preaching was based on the idea that a preacher must get a proposition before he can build a sermon. To stress his concept, he compared the parts of a sermon to a tree: the roots being the text; the trunk being the proposition; and the limbs and branches being the expansion of the sermon.[1] The proposition does provide the base for the development of the sermon. It also condenses the larger development. By this we mean the outline is the proposition expanded, and the proposition is the outline condensed. Sound structure and even affective delivery depend upon a clear proposition. Charles W. Koller described the proposition as "the heart of the sermon."[2] Consider then three reasons why the proposition is a necessity in the building of a sermon.

(1) A proposition is necessary because out of it every part of the sermon will unfold. Having a good proposition solves one prominent problem of sermon preparation, and that is, How do I even begin to build a sermon? You begin your sermon with a simple sentence which we

call a *proposition*. Out of the proposition will come major divisions. Also, the proposition will be the dominant factor in selecting substance material for the sermon.

(2) A proposition is necessary because it is a unifying factor for a sermon. Building a helpful biblical sermon depends on having one point, a whole, not a collection of alien particles. Each part of the sermon will gravitate to the proposition, thus aiding in securing unity in a sermon.

(3) A proposition is necessary because it enhances the communication of a sermon. Good communication happens when the speaker knows where he is going and the hearers can follow him. Only when a proposition is clear in your mind can you speak to the point. When this has been accomplished in preparation, you know where you are going in delivering the sermon. Therefore, the proposition is vital both in preparing and in delivering the sermon. When you get a good biblical idea in your mind which relates to people's needs, you can then develop, expand, support, and illustrate. When you know where you are going, your people will be able to follow with greater understanding.

The qualities of a proposition. Because of the importance of the proposition, you need to learn its best qualities.

(1) The first significant quality of a proposition is singleness of expression. This is the reason why the proposition must be a simple sentence in the present or the future tense. Compound or complex sentences create several ideas. A simple sentence states one idea, hence you will have singleness of expression.

(2) The second quality of a proposition is congruity with the text. The proposition and the text relate inseparably to each other. Let us look again at the illustration of the tree. The text is the root. The proposition is the trunk. The branches and leaves are the sermon

parts. Yet, the tree is one entity. Using the analogy of the tree, we can see that the root and trunk have an inseparable relationship. The same should be true of the text and the proposition.

(3) A third quality of a good proposition is its capability for development. There will be many important matters which need to emerge from the proposition. There might be a series of declarations which amplify its meaning. There could be a series of significant reasons why the proposition is true. Or, there might be a series of implications that follow from the proposition. Whatever the case, the proposition must be capable of development. If, after careful study and thought, you cannot derive ideas from the proposition, you need to work on another one.

(4) A fourth quality of a good proposition is its simplicity. You should strive to state a clear, unambiguous proposition. If you state the proposition in a simple sentence in fifteen words or less, it will not likely be loaded with embellishments or exaggerations. Keep your proposition as simple as possible.

The types of propositions. The proposition may be stated in a variety of ways. The way you prepare and state the proposition will be governed generally by your objective or what you want people to do as a result of your sermon. We want to share with you six different types of propositions. Also, we shall illustrate how all six types could be prepared from one text, namely Genesis 5:24: "Enoch walked with God."

(1) You may prepare a *possibility proposition*. This will be a statement which gives an attainable goal in a person's life. It will express an optimistic outlook. The possibility proposition of Genesis 5:24 would be: You can have a closer walk with God.

(2) A second type of proposition you might want to prepare is a *predictive proposition*. This is the kind

which foretells what will happen in a person's life. An example stated from Genesis 5:24 is: Your life will be blessed when you walk with God.

(3) Another type of proposition is the *persuasive proposition.* This is one which is an inducement to believe or to do something. Again using Genesis 5:24, the example would be: God calls you to walk with him.

(4) You may also prepare a *comparative proposition.* This will be a proposition which discloses differences or similarities. From the positive statement of Genesis 5:24, you might make the following comparison: Walking with God differs from walking away from God.

(5) A fifth type is the *evaluative proposition.* This ascertains the value or benefit of an action. Using Genesis 5:24, you may get an evaluative proposition which is: Walking with God is the best way to live.

(6) A sixth type of proposition, which will be used frequently, is the *declarative proposition.* This is a statement of fact. One declarative proposition of Genesis 5:24 would be: Walking with God means to obey him.

You can see that there are many ways to state a proposition. There are many ways to look at a truth of Scripture or at the needs of people. Of course all texts will not have all six of the possibilities of Genesis 5:24. More than likely the particular type of proposition you state will be determined by your personality, by the Holy Spirit's illumination to your particular personality, by your insight into the text, and by the needs of your people. Each proposition type will suggest a slightly different type of development for the sermon.

The examples of propositions. You will need to learn how to prepare a proposition. Your ETS and your knowledge and association with people will help you with this process. Work on the art of stating your sermon idea in a simple sentence in present or future tense. We want to furnish five examples of the proposition. The text, ETS, and the proposition will be stated together so you might see the interrelationship of these parts.

(1) **Text**: Genesis 5:24
    ETS: Enoch walked with God.
    Proposition: You can walk with God.

(2) **Text**: Mark 2:1-12
    ETS: Jesus helped a paralyzed man.
    Proposition: Jesus helps people with their needs.

(3) **Text**: Ephesians 2:1-10
    ETS: Paul described Christians as God's workmanship.
    Proposition: Christians are God's masterpieces.

(4) **Text**: James 1:19-26
    ETS: James taught Christians how to respond properly to God's Word.
    Proposition: We need to use the Bible correctly.

(5) **Text**: Philippians 1:19-26
    ETS: Paul faced the reality of his death.
    Proposition: Christians face death too.

From our discussion of the proposition and from the examples, we want to review with you the pertinent facts about a proposition.

(1) The proposition is a simple sentence either in the present or future tense which has no more that fifteen words.

(2) The proposition should have a vital relationship to the text and to the needs of people.

(3) The proposition may take many forms: possibility, predictive, persuasive, comparative, evaluative, or declarative. Some propositions could be stated in all six forms.

(4) The proposition results from a careful study of the Bible and of people.

(5) The proposition moves you to the body, introduction, substance material, and the conclusion of the sermon.

(6) The proposition should possess the capability for expansion.

When the art of getting an ETS and ESS has been mastered, you have a good start toward the building of a sermon. Before you proceed any further in reading and studying this book, these principles must be mastered. Practice stating an ETS and an ESS for awhile. When you feel relatively comfortable with these two sentences, you will be ready for the art of stating your objective for the sermon.

Notes

1. Austin Phelps, *The Theory of Preaching: Lectures on Homiletics* (New York: Charles Scribner's Sons, 1881), p. 308.
2. Charles W. Koller, *Expository Preaching Without Notes* (Grand Rapids, Michigan: Baker Book House, 1962), pp. 72-75.

5
Directing the Sermon Idea to Action

Benjamin R. Lacy once told of an incident in the early part of his ministry. One Saturday night Lacy proceeded to read his Sunday morning sermon to his wife. When he had finished reading, Mrs. Lacy asked, "Ben, *why* are you going to preach that sermon?" Lacy confessed that the question first made him angry, but it forced him back to the study for more sermon preparation. In the study he asked himself the same question that his wife had posed, "Just why am I going to preach this sermon?" He had not raised that question either before or during the sermon-building process. After his long hours of sermon preparation, he could find no reason which seemed adequate to justify his preaching the sermon. Lacy began to prepare another sermon with a clear and specific objective. If anyone asked him the question, "Why are you going to preach that sermon?" he would have a specific answer.[1]

Prior to preparation of the sermon the wise sermon builder determines what he wants people to do as a result of hearing the sermon. Having a clear objective in mind gives incentive to your labors, for you know that the sermon will be directed to people's needs. Harry Emerson Fosdick noted that the difference between a sermon and a lecture was that a lecture elucidated a subject, and a sermon was concerned with an objective to be achieved.

Having no specific objective is a fatal flaw for sermon preparation. The sermon may contain exacting biblical interpretation, symmetrical homiletical structure, and brilliant use of language, but without a clear, specific objective all of these matters will not be directed toward behavorial changes in a person's life. Lack of a clearly defined objective in a sermon could explain why some people remark as they leave worship, "What the preacher said was well said, but I don't know what he wanted me to do."

Having a clear objective for each sermon comprises a basic requirement for sermon preparation. Sermons are not built for listening only, but they are to produce action in the lives of people. The preacher who has a definite objective to reach in a sermon sees in the distance the point to which he wants to travel and consequently seeks various means to accomplish the objective. The materials he selects for the sermon will be determined by the objective. The objective answers the question, Why am I going to preach this sermon? It is a statement of what you want your people to do as a result of the sermon. You want to build a sermon which will call persons to a decision, to a commitment which leads to a change in behavior.

Your objective will be a simple sentence of fifteen words or less. It will guide you in the preparation and in the delivery of the sermon. Sometimes your objective may come before either the text, ETS, or ESS. This more than likely happens when you observe a person's need. In such instances you need to select an appropriate text, summarize the text with an ETS, and write the ESS. In order to learn how to get an objective for a sermon, let us consider the general purposes of preaching, the three domains of the sermon, and the specific sermon objective.

The General Purposes of Preaching

Before studying the specific objective for a sermon, we need to investigate the general purposes of preaching. H. Grady Davis described three general purposes for preaching: proclamation *(kerussein)*, teaching *(didaskein)*, and therapy *(therapeuein)*. According to Davis the general purposes of preaching in the New Testament times were threefold: proclamation involved announcing the good news about Jesus Christ to the unconverted; teaching imparted various truths on the basis of the gospel; and therapy sought to improve the condition of people based on their experience with the good news.[2]

You may discover these and other general purposes of preaching by studying New Testament preaching and by observing the needs of people. There is no limit to the number of purposes in preaching because people will always have diverse needs. In our study of the Bible and in our association with people, we have summarized four general and prominent purposes of preaching: evangelistic, growth, relational, and therapeutic.

The evangelistic purpose. A prominent purpose of New Testament preaching was the proclamation of the good news so that people would repent and would trust Christ. Jesus, the model preacher, preached in order that people might repent and enter the kingdom of God. "Now after that John was put in prison, Jesus came into Galilee, preaching the gospel of the kingdom of God, and saying, The time is fulfilled, and the kingdom of God is at hand: repent ye, and believe the gospel" (Mark 1:14-15). The apostles and other New Testament preachers announced the news of what God had done in Jesus Christ. Upon the basis of the message, calls were made for repentance and faith. They preached with a purpose in mind, namely to open life to the Lord. Without a doubt the New Testament preachers had an evangelistic purpose for their sermons.

You will have an evangelistic purpose for many sermons. You will announce the good news about Jesus Christ as the fulfillment of Old Testament prophecy, his life and ministry, his death and resurrection, his exaltation, and his final return. The evangelistic purpose undergirds all the other purposes of preaching. For example, in sermons on prayer, you would seek to make people aware that "in Christ" a person learns to pray. All of the other three purposes—growth, relational, and therapeutic—rest on the basis of a person being a Christian.

The growth purpose. Another prominent purpose of New Testament preachers was the growth of the converts in Christ. The Lord urged people to enter the kingdom when he preached, "The kingdom of God is at hand: repent ye," (Mark 1:15). Growing disciples into qualitative kingdom people comprised a large part of the Lord's preaching and teaching. His Sermon on the Mount was addressed to disciples who needed to grow as kingdom people. The other New Testament preachers, such as Peter and Paul, had a maturation purpose in their proclamation. Without a doubt the New Testament preachers had a teaching purpose in their sermons.

Relating the gospel to life should be a prominent purpose in preaching today. Christians want and need to understand more about their faith in Christ. Some sermons will be directed primarily to believers for the purpose of maturing their Christian life. Christians grow when they learn the doctrines (teachings) of Christianity and when they apply these doctrines to life. Preaching on the great Christian doctrines helps people in their pilgrimage toward a mature faith. You cannot neglect the evangelistic purpose of securing converts, and you cannot neglect their growth when they become Christians.

The relational purpose. The specific thrust of the relational purpose in preaching is to build, to enhance, to strengthen, or to mend relationships. Throughout his earthly ministry Jesus emphasized in his preaching and teaching a threefold relationship—with God, with the world, and with each other. The apostles and other New

Testament preachers preached so that people might live more effectively in their relationships with others.

Helping Christians live in good relationships with Christ, other Christians, and the world is a worthy purpose for preaching today. The gospel can apply to the areas where people touch the lives of other people—family, business, school, marketplace, and other areas.

The therapeutic purpose. Studying biblical preaching reveals a therapeutic purpose. Jesus preached to help people with their hurts. The first sermon of Jesus' ministry was delivered at the synagogue in Nazareth. The Lord preached the sermon with a therapeutic purpose in mind.

The Spirit of the Lord is upon me, because he hath anointed me to preach the gospel to the poor; he hath sent me to heal the brokenhearted, to preach deliverance to the captives, and recovering of sight to the blind, to set at liberty them that are bruised, to preach the acceptable year of the Lord (Luke 4:18-19).

Jesus sought to cure people of their personal plights. New Testament preachers also had a therapeutic purpose. They wanted to help heal human hurts with their sermons.

Today's preachers need a therapeutic purpose in their preaching. Myriads of the problems beset people—guilt, advancing years, bereavement, fear, anxiety, depression, disappointment, sickness, financial loss, low self-esteem, loneliness, boredom, and others. You want to build sermons for the purpose of helping people to secure healing in Christ. As you study the Bible and listen to people, you will be impressed to preach sermons in order to help with human hurts.

The Different Domains of the Sermon

A sermon which meets the needs of people has an objective. But what kind of objective should the sermon have? Should a sermon be prepared to inform people? Should a sermon be prepared to create feelings? The answers to these last two questions are yes and no. Yes, because you do want to inform and to incite feelings. No, because neither the information nor the feelings are the ultimate objectives for a sermon. You want a specific objective which calls for action.

The art of building and delivering a sermon has been applied to other areas such as hermeneutics, communication, and psychology. Studies in education programs have heightened interest in teaching. Kibler, Barker, Miles, and Cegala in their book *Objectives for Instruction and Evaluation* summarized the three domains for teaching objectives as cognitive, affective, and psychomotor. The cognitive domain relates to the intellect; the affective domain encompasses the feelings; and the psychomotor domain refers to action. These educational ideas will be applied to the priorities of objectives in sermons.

The cognitive domain: knowledge. Imparting information is necessary in building and in delivering a sermon. This is not the ultimate domain though. Knowledge about the text and the sermon idea is necessary if you are to have any hope of achieving a specific objective. Imparting facts about the Bible and relating these facts to people's needs would be a necessary cognitive domain. Calling for people to act upon the basis of the message would be the ultimate reason for the cognitive domain. Knowledge will be used as a process of inviting people to act on some part of God's Word.

You will share factual or cognitive information. In doing so, you are laying the foundation for calling people to action. The ultimate goal for your sermon is not the transmission of information but the transformation of people. Abundant information will be given in a sermon through biblical data, illustrations, outlines, explanations, narrations, and other means. However, you neither prepare nor deliver a sermon in order that people may merely know the data. The cognitive domain is necessary in order to get to the place where you persuade people to act upon the facts.

Let us give an example from the sermon, "Walking with God" based on Genesis 5:24. You would prepare data on Enoch and information regarding the biblical expression "walked with God." This data would be used to persuade people to walk with God. Without the information, little basis could be established to urge people to walk with God. As a specific objective—"I want people to know what it means to walk with God"—would be an incomplete objective. It would not be in the ultimate domain for a specific sermon objective. You will want your hearers to gain knowledge, but you want to achieve more than this. A better objective would be—"I want people to live each day according to God's way."

The affective domain: emotion. Emotions are subjective feelings produced when a person considers a situation, an object, or a person in relationship to himself. The content, design, and delivery of material in the cognitive (knowledge) domain should be such as to aid in achieving success in the affective area. That is to say, effective communication of quality sermon material will help arouse a favorable feeling for the message proclaimed.

We are concerned that sermons affect the feelings of people in a constructive manner. In order for this to happen the feeling must be in the person preparing and delivering the sermon. Charles Silvester Horne said it in this way: "Nobody ought ever to go into a pulpit who can think and talk about sin and salvation and the Cross of Christ . . . without profound emotion and passion."[3]

Arousing people's emotions is an important domain for preaching. But, it is not the preeminent domain. Favorable emotional responses lead to desirable actions. Now we can move to the top priority in stating an objective for a sermon.

The psychomotor domain: action. Writers on educational objectives define the psychomotor domain as the desire for skill and performance. In other words teachers would impart information and incite favorable feelings toward the material so the student could apply the facts. This could easily be related to preaching. No objective for a sermon stands higher than that of achieving action. Imparting information is important. Arousing emotions has its proper place. However, the preeminent objective for a sermon is the one which incorporates the factual and the emotional domains in persuading people to be and to do something.

Now we are ready to give attention to this preeminent psychomotor domain. We call this the specific objective for a sermon.

The Specific Sermon Objective

Up to this point you have learned to select a sermon idea, to summarize the text (ETS), to project a proposition (ESS), and to recognize cognitive and affective domains for the sermon. Now you are ready to study carefully what we call the sermon's "Specific Objective."

The concept of an objective. The specific objective is one that calls for action based on the authority of the text. It is a simple sentence of fifteen words or less stated either in the present or future tense. It answers the question, Why am I preparing this sermon?

As we have stated earlier, the objective might come to your mind and heart before the text, the ETS, or the proposition. If so, write the objective in the psychomotor domain and then work to get a text, an ETS, and a proposition. Usually an objective will come to you when you see needs in the lives of people and you want those needs met with your sermons. For example, you might see the need to help people in your church with their numerous trials. You have seen their troubles. They have told you their problems. This would lead you to have an objective in the psychomotor domain. It could be — "I want to help people live constructively with their troubles." When your objective was in mind, obviously you would turn to securing a text and to preparing a proposition. If the text, ETS, and the proposition precede the objective, then prepare a specific objective.

The qualities of an objective. The specific objective has several desirable qualities.

(1) The first of these is to be specific. Vagueness here will show in both the preparation and the delivery of the sermon. The same is true when multiple objectives are given equal importance. This will hamper your efforts to achieve action. The tendency with some is to deal in generalities. Sometimes the impression is made that the primary concern of the preacher was on what he was doing and how he was doing it. The primary concern should be on what you are trying to achieve in the lives of those who hear. We are fully aware of the fact that the Holy Spirit does the achieving. However, isn't it true that when he has led us in building a sermon to meet a specific need, we become better instruments for his use? For example, using an objective — "I want the audience to be good stewards" — seems to be too general. A more specific objective would be — "I want people to use their time wisely" or "I want people to tithe their income."

(2) A second desirable quality of an objective is attainability. The objective should be a goal which the audience can attain by human response to God's power. Oftentimes people get discouraged when you aim too high. When an objective is achieved, you and your people move on to attaining another objective. It is better to attain a reachable objective than to fail completely because the objective was too big and thus not attainable. People come to achieve larger objectives by first achiev-

ing smaller, more readily attainable objectives. An unat-
tainable objective would be—"I want my people to have
all their problems solved and their needs met as a result
of this sermon." A more attainable objective would
be—"I want the audience to have victory today over the
temptation to be unkind to others."

(3) A third quality of a sermon objective is measurability. This trait is closely akin to the matter of attain-
ment. Ability to discern the extent of the influence of a
sermon is difficult. Measurability begins by thinking
about reaching your goal even as you are working out
your objective. Your hearers will be able to measure
degrees of growth as a result of applying the objective to
their lives. So, you need to prepare an objective which
could be measured. The effect of a sermon on tithing
could be assessed. Did the hearers begin to tithe? The
effect of a sermon on handling grief could be determined.
Did those who grieve find help to cope with the crisis?
Objectives will need to be written so that a degree of
measurement may be discerned.

Writing an objective for a sermon at the beginning of
the building process requires discipline. The first at-
tempts will be difficult. Experienced pastors testify
though that the fruit of the discipline is worth the effort.
Try to write what you want people to do as a result of
your preparing and preaching the sermon. Make this
objective specific, attainable, and measurable.

The importance of an objective. Why do you need to
be so concerned about an objective for your sermon? Is it
really that important? Yes, we consider the objective to
be the process where you relate to the needs of people.
Consequently, on one hand, the objective is important
for the preacher. It guides you in the preparation of the
sermon. When you have a specific objective, then all
material will be gathered with this in mind. Only the
structural form and material that will help achieve the
objective will be used. On the other hand, the objective

will affect the hearers. They will discern that you are
expecting action. Sometimes people will decide immediately to act. At other times results will come over the
years. Do not neglect the objective. It is important for
you and for your people.

The examples of objectives. In two other stages of
sermon construction (ETS and ESS), we have furnished
examples. Using the same texts we had for ETS and
ESS we now give examples of specific sermon objectives:

(1) Text: Genesis 5:24
     Topic: The Best Exercise
     ETS: Enoch walked with God.
     Proposition: You can walk with God.
     Objective: My objective is for my hearers to live
     each day according to God's way.
(2) Text: Mark 2:1-12
     Topic: The Miracle Worker
     ETS: Jesus helped a paralyzed man.
     Proposition: Jesus helps people with their needs.
     Objective: My objective is for people to experience
     Jesus' help in their lives.
(3) Text: Ephesians 2:1-10
     Topic: God's Masterpiece
     ETS: Paul described Christians as God's work-
     manship.
     Proposition: Christians are God's masterpieces.
     Objective: My objective is to persuade people to
     allow God to shape their lives.
(4) Text: James 1:19-26
     Topic: How to Use the Bible
     ETS: James taught believers how to respond prop-
     erly to God's Word.
     Proposition: We need to use the Bible correctly.
     Objective: My objective is to help Christians to use
     the Bible according to God's instructions.

(5)   **Text:** Philippians 1:19-26
     Topic: Facing Your Death
     ETS: Paul faced the reality of his death.
     Proposition: Christians face death too.
     Objective: My objective is to prepare people for death.

From our discussion of the objective and from the above examples, we want to remind you of the following facts.

(1) The objective is a simple sentence of fifteen words or less in the present or future tense.

(2) The objective for your sermon will be in the psychomotor domain (action) even though you will deal with the cognitive and affective domains.

(3) The objective will be stated as an action which you want your hearers to accomplish.

(4) The objective may come first in the process, it may come later, but it must come if you want to help people.

The practice of using a specific objective with each sermon will strengthen your efforts in helping people. We urge you to refrain from yielding to the temptation to design sermons with no specific objective in mind. So, practice using a specific objective for each sermon. It will strengthen your efforts of helping people.

Notes

1. Donald G. Miller, *The Way to Biblical Preaching* (New York: Abingdon Press, 1957), p. 112.

2. H. Grady Davis, *Design for Preaching* (Philadelphia: Fortress Press, 1958), pp. 98-138.

3. Charles Silvester Horne, *The Romance of Preaching* (New York: Fleming H. Revell Company, 1914), p. 256.

6
Developing the Sermon

The preacher who wishes to help people with his sermons needs good structure. Not everyone is pleased with the thought of structuring a sermon. Some disdain the mention of the words *outline* or *structure*. They feel that significant ideas are what really matter and the way you put them across is of little importance. Therefore, these preachers do not make an effort to structure any idea they want to communicate. This seriously impedes the effectiveness of their communication. Formlessness is not the best design for a sermon.

Perhaps others are too mechanical when it comes to the idea of structure. These preachers conceive of a sermon mainly in connection with points, subpoints, and sub-subpoints. Such a preacher has a tendency to get lost in the points and subpoints, and he fails to understand or to communicate the main point of the sermon. Clyde Fant labels overemphasis on structure as "neo-scholastic preaching."[1]

If neither formlessness nor overemphasis on form are best for building a sermon, what do you do in order to build a sermon? One answer is—you develop the proposition. By getting an ETS you have a biblical stance. By getting a proposition you have a contemporary stance. The major divisions unfold from the proposition by using a probing question and a unifying word. When the structure comes from a proposition, the results seem to be more holistic. The development focuses upon the one

81

idea in the proposition. Obviously then, structuring the sermons begins with major divisions. This will mean that the whole will be greater than the sum of its parts (holistic). You use structure in such a way that it doesn't call attention to itself but does make understanding easier. Harry Emerson Fosdick called the structure of a sermon "organized thinking." Without a doubt some preachers have been effective without structure in their sermons, but they have possessed extraordinary compensating strengths. Perhaps their sermons would have been more effective if there had been structural excellence also. Having a clearly stated proposition guides you in further thought, holds you to one idea, assures balance in the message, and keeps the message moving.

Functional structure not only helps the preacher but helps the audience as well. Without logical organization in a sermon, communication is impaired. This is true of the message as a whole, a sentence, or even a single word. For example, the letters I-L-B-E-B in that order communicate nothing, but the ordered letters B-I-B-L-E communicate a word. That which is true of a word can be true of the organization of the sermon. Good organization helps the hearers to follow progressively your thinking. Try recalling a list of random numbers: 5,13,4,6,112,3,7,219,86. Getting a logical reason for this ordering is baffling. Now try a list of logically, ordered numbers: 2,4,6,8,10,12,14,16,18,20,22. You can see logic, and you can follow this arrangement. You can also remember the design. Structure is far more than show. It has a function. Good structure is used to help you proclaim one idea for the people. It is a means of helping the audience understand the message, follow it, and act responsibly in daily living.

If structure is so important, how do you achieve it? Do you get random ideas and arrange them symmetrically? The obvious answer is no. To structure a sermon you get a proposition and then probe the proposition. The major divisions will unfold. For help in developing the sermon, we shall discuss probing the proposition, unfolding the proposition, and expanding the proposition.

Probing the Proposition

How do you get structure from a proposition? The answer is that you will use homiletical devices, such as the probing question and the unifying word. With the ETS, ESS, and the objective in mind, you may proceed to the exciting task of probing the proposition.

The probing questions. The proposition may be developed by selecting one of several probing questions. You may even put most of these questions to the proposition before determining which one you will use. However, only one question will be used for a given sermon. The particular question you select will be determined by what you want to accomplish and the situation of your people at the time. The three most frequently used questions are what, why, and how.

(1) What? Probing the proposition with *what* would introduce a sequence of meanings, truths, facts, implications, definitions, particulars, characteristics, inclusions, or exclusions.

(2) Why? Questioning the proposition with *why* would introduce reasons or objectives for the main divisions.

(3) How? Interrogating the proposition with *how* would introduce a sequence of ways.

In addition to these three questions, there are four other probing questions. You will find these to be used less for developing a sermon.

(4) Who? or Whom? Inquiry with these forms of interrogatives yield answers of persons to be enumerated, identified, classified, or included.

(5) Which? Asking this question suggests a series of choices, objects, or alternatives.

(6) When? Using this as a probing question suggests times, phases, or conditions.

(7) Where? Asking this question introduces a sequence of places or sources. As we have said, several probing questions may be tried to see which suits a particular need best, but please remember that only one will finally be chosen. Now we are ready to help you ask the one question to the proposition.

The one question. While all seven of the above questions may be put to a proposition for study purposes, you will select only one for a particular sermon. The selection of the probing question will be determined by the condition of your people and what you want to accomplish in the sermon. If you feel your people are not informed sufficiently on a topic, you will probe the proposition with *what* which leads to a unifying word such as *truths*. If you feel your people have sufficient facts about a subject, but they lack motivation, then you would use the question *why* which leads to the unifying word *reasons*. Then if you feel they have sufficient facts and compelling motivation but do not know how, then you would probe the proposition with *how* which would lead to the unifying word *ways*. The particular probing question you choose will be influenced by the needs of your people and by the specific sermon objective. Sometimes your people may need to know the *what* of an idea. Again, they may know the what, but they do not know *why* they should be involved. Then again, they may know both the *what* and the *why*, but they do not know the *how* of it.

We want to give you an example of the probing process of the three most frequently used questions. These examples will furnish you insight into how you may get three different developments from one proposition by simply changing the probing question.

Text: Acts 1:1-8 (1:8 focal verse)

ETS: The early Christians were commissioned to be involved meaningfully in missions.

Proposition: Christians should be involved meaningfully in missions.

Objective: My objective is to get my people involved meaningfully in missions.

Suppose our people are not informed sufficiently about the meaning of missions. We would probe the proposition with *what* and the unifying word would be *truths* about missions.

Each major division would be a truth coming out of the question and the unifying word. Let us notice an example of the process:

Probing Question: What is missions?
Unifying Word: *Truths*
Transitional Sentence: Let us notice some biblical *truths* about missions.
  I. The first truth is that God wants to save the world.
  II. The second truth is that God wants to use every believer in saving the world.
  III. The third truth is that God wants to give power for missions.

Suppose your people are sufficiently informed about missions but not motivated to be involved personally. The probing question could be put to the same proposition, and the unifying word *reasons* could be used.

Probing Question: Why should Christians be involved?
Unifying Word: *Reasons*
Transitional Sentence: Let us examine some *reasons* why Christians should be involved in missions.
  I. The first reason is that the Lord commands missions involvement.
  II. The second reason is that the world needs missions involvement.
  III. The third reason is that the Holy Spirit empowers for missions involvement.

With the two questions *what* and *why,* you have constructed two sermons from the same proposition. The difference in emphasis has been influenced by the particular situation of your people. Now move to another possible probe of the proposition. If your people are sufficiently informed and are motivated adequately, but they do not know what to do, you might put the question *how* to the proposition. It will suggest biblical *ways* to be involved in missions.

Probing Question: How can Christians be involved meaningfully in missions?
Unifying Word: *Ways*
Transitional Sentence: Let us apply some *ways* that Christians may be involved meaningfully in missions.
  I. The first way is to offer prayer support.
  II. The second way is to send others.
  III. The third way is to give money.
  IV. The fourth way is to witness where we live.

In this exercise with Acts 1:1-8 we did not put the other four probing questions to the proposition, for they did not seem appropriate for this particular proposition. So, you see that in order to choose the right question to the proposition, you will need to know your text and to know where your people are in relationship to the proposition. In the process of choosing the right question, you might want to probe the proposition with three or more questions. Each probing question will allow the possibility of a different sermon. Going through the probing process with three or more questions helps you select the appropriate question most helpful for the hearers. Furthermore, you will be helped by this probing process, for it helps you amplify the meaning of the text and proposition, as well as suggest several sermon possibilities for the same text.

The unifying word. One of the most helpful homiletical devices is the unifying word. The unifying word ties together each main division, thus it guarantees unity. Each unifying word is always a plural noun or a plural noun form of a verb. In the plural form, the unifying word covers all the major divisions, and in the singular the unifying word distinguishes each major division. For example, in the above illustration where the question, How can Christians be involved meaningfully in missions? was asked, the unifying word was *ways*. It described the nature of all divisions *(ways)*, and each division was a *way* to be involved in missions.

The range of unifying words is unlimited. We shall furnish a starter list. You will add continuously to the list as the need arises. The use of a good thesaurus or collection of English synonyms or antonyms will be helpful.

A Starter List of Unifying Words

abuses	barriers	concessions	disciplines
accusations	beginnings	conclusions	disclosures
actions	beliefs	conditions	discoveries
acts	benefits	consequences	distinctions
actualities	blessings	contrasts	doctrines
admonitions	burdens	corrections	duties
advantages		credentials	
affairs	calls	criteria	elements
affirmations	causes	customs	encouragements
agreements	certainties		essentials
aims	challenges	declarations	estimates
alternatives	changes	defenses	events
assertions	charges	deficiencies	evidences
angles	claims	definitions	evils
answers	clues	degrees	examples
applications	commitments	demands	exchanges
assumptions	comparisons	denials	exclamations
assurances	compensations	devices	exhortations
attainments	compromises	differences	expectations
attitudes	compulsions	directions	experiences
attributes	conceptions	directives	expressions

facets

factors

facts

failures

faults

favors

fears

features

finalities

forces

functions

fundamentals

gains

generalizations

gifts

graces

groups

handicaps

hopes

hungers

ideas

imperatives

implications

impressions

improvements

impulses

incentives

incidents

indictments

inferences

injunctions

insights

inspirations

instances

instructions

instruments

intimations

invitations

items

joys

judgments

justifications

kinds

lessons

levels

liabilities

losses

loyalties

manifestations

marks

methods

mistakes

moments

motives

movements

mysteries

needs

notions

objections

observations

obstacles

offers

omissions

opinions

opportunities

particulars

peculiarities

penalties

perils

phases

phrases

pledges

points

possitilities

practices

premises

prerogative

principles

priorities

probabilities

problems

processes

promises

promptings

pronouncements

proofs

prophecies

propositions

provisions

qualifications

qualities

questions

realities

realizations

reasons

reflections

refusals

remarks

remedies

reminders

requirements

reservations

resources

responses

restraints

results

revelations

rewards

risks

rules

safeguards

satisfactions

secrets

sins

sources

specifications

statements

steps

stipulations

successes

suggestions

superlatives

suppositions

surprises

symptoms

tendencies

testimonies

tests

thoughts

threats

topics

totalities

truths

urges

uses

values

views

violations

virtues

voices

warnings

ways

weaknesses

words

You can see that we used the unifying word in each major division of the examples from Acts 1:8. This is to say that when the unifying word was *truths,* each major division was *a truth;* when the unifying word was *reasons,* each major division was *a reason;* and when the unifying word was *ways,* each major division was a *way.* Thus, each division was linked with the unifying word, and all divisions were tied together by it. As you begin the method of building a sermon you might want to use the unifying word in each major division, but its use is not necessary. In our subsequent examples, we shall not use the unifying word in the major divisions, but it will be tied closely to them.

The unifying word will be used in the transitional sentence which links the introduction with the outline. The use of other transitions will be discussed in the next chapter. The following transitional sentence will help you to see this matter: Let us notice some biblical *truths* about missions.

Unfolding the Proposition

By now you should see that major divisions unfold from the proposition. You will use the homiletical devices of a probing question and a unifying word to produce major divisions. In referring to major divisions, we shall use interchangeably the words *outline, structure,* or *design.* Most outlines contain from two to five major divisions which relate to the proposition. In teaching the process of unfolding the proposition, we shall discuss the mechanics of major divisions, the qualities of major divisions, and the examples of major divisions.

The mechanics of major divisions. Getting an outline seems to be a hard process for most preachers. You may ask, How can I construct my own outline rather than borrowing another preacher's outline? The problem related to the mechanics of getting major divisions can be solved by asking one probing question which produces a unifying word. This in turn unfolds the proposition into logical, natural divisions. Whether you want to use the unifying word in the statement of the major division is optional. However, each major division must answer to the unifying word in order to guarantee unity. This process helps you get your own outline.

In the mechanics of getting the outline from the proposition, the text can be useful. Sometimes you can get each major division directly from the text. This would be a natural source, for the ETS and the ESS will be related closely to the text. We want to demonstrate one example of how you may get major divisions directly from the text.

Text: Ephesians 2:1-10
Topic: God's Masterpiece
ETS: Paul described Christians as God's workmanship.
Proposition: Christians are God's masterpieces.
Objective: My objective is to persuade people to allow God to shape their lives.
Probing Question: What does the text disclose about God's masterpiece?
Unifying Word: *Disclosures*
Transitional Sentence: Let us study the *disclosures* of the text about God's masterpiece.
Outline:
 I. God works with an impossible product. 2:1-3.
 II. God works with an incredible power. 2:4-6
 III. God works with indomitable purpose. 2:7-10

You can see that the major divisions (I, II, III) came as answers to the probing question addressed to the proposition. The answers were contained directly in the text (I—2:1-3; II—2:4-6; III—2:7-10). A good rule of thumb is to look first for the answers to your probing question in the text. Also, you might want to keep your divisions, in most cases, in the order found in the text. Though rearrangement of verses is permissable, you need to proceed with care. An example of changing the order of verses is as follows:

Text: James 1:2-12
Topic: The Trials of Our Lives
ETS: James discussed the hardships of life.
Proposition: Christians have to deal with the troubles of life.
Objective: My objective is to help people master life's hardships.
Probing Question: How do Christians deal with the troubles of life?
Unifying Word: *Ways*
Transitional Sentence: Let us notice the *ways* Christians can deal with trials.
Outline:
   I. Christians acknowledge the variety of trials. 1:2,9-11
   II. Christians seek God's help for trials. 1:5,6-8
   III. Christians rejoice in the dividends of trials. 1:3-4

You will observe that each division answered the probing question which was addressed to the proposition. The answers came from the text, but they were not in consecutive order.

Deriving major divisions from the text is not the same as the running commentary approach. In the running commentary approach you go from verse to verse, explaining, proving, and illustrating without the development of a single idea.

In the mechanics of getting the outline from the proposition, you can use the text to suggest the major divisions. Each major division does not have to come directly from the text. They can be suggested by the text. The divisions will be biblical, for you have developed your proposition from the text. We want to demonstrate one example of the mechanics of getting major divisions indirectly from the text.

Topic: Slaves for Christ Jesus
ETS: James called himself a bondslave of Jesus Christ.
Proposition: Christians are slaves of Jesus Christ.
Objective: My objective is that hearers will act as God's slaves.
Unifying Word: *Meanings*
Transitional Sentence: Let us notice some *meanings* of being God's slave.
Outline:
    I. Being a slave means absolute ownership.
   II. Being a slave means unquestioning obedience.
  III. Being a slave means implicit trust.
  IV. Being a slave means undivided loyalty.

You can see that none of the divisions came directly from the text. Each division unfolded from the question. What does it mean to be God's slave? The text was used directly.

Major divisions emerge directly or indirectly from the text. In either case, the mechanical process is the same—probe the proposition, and the answers are the major divisions. Unite the major divisions with a unifying word. Be careful about getting major divisions by analyzing the text, for it could become a running commentary on Scripture without one focal idea. Furthermore, be careful about drawing major divisions from the text indirectly, for you could depart easily from the intention and the meaning of the text.

The qualities of major divisions. Like the other processes of sermon building which we have considered, you will want to work for quality in major divisions. From our perspective the outline needs to have several discernable qualities.

(1) Good major divisions are coextensive with the

proposition. Each major division needs to relate directly back to the proposition.

(2) Good major divisions are stated as simple sentences either in the present or future tense. Putting major divisions in the past tense could hinder application. In our opinion, you would profit by avoiding the past tense for major divisions.

(3) Good major divisions are united. Although a sermon will have two or more major divisions, actually it will develop one idea. Each major division unfolds from the proposition by a probing question, and the divisions are linked to each other by the unifying word. Unity requires that the divisions relate back to the proposition.

(4) The best outline has parallel construction. If the first division is a declarative sentence, the remaining divisions will be declarative sentences. We feel that a uniformity is best in placing the words in sequence. This is to say that the second, third, fourth, or fifth divisions need the same kind of word order as the first division.

(5) Each major division is stated independently. Divisions need to be kept mutually exclusive. Each division is distinct from the other divisions, yet interrelated to each other.

(6) Good major divisions are proportionately balanced. Divisions should be given comparable proportions of treatment. The first division should not be excessively longer than the other divisions or vice versa.

Let us look at an example.

Text: Psalm 19:1-14
Topic: God's Multi-Communication
ETS: The psalmist discussed some ways that God speaks to people.
ESS: God is speaking to us.
Objective: My objective is to urge people to listen for God's command.

Probing Question: How does God speak to us?

Unifying Word: *Ways*

Transitional Sentence: Let us notice some *ways* God speaks to us.

Outline:

    I. God speaks through nature. 19:1-6

   II. God speaks by his Word. 19:7-11

  III. God speaks in our life experiences. 19:12-14

In reference to the above outline ask yourself the questions:

    —Are the divisions faithful to the text and to people's needs?

    —Are the divisions in simple sentences?

    —Do the divisions have unity?

    —Are the divisions simple enough for most people to understand?

    —Do the divisions have parallelism?

    —Are the divisions mutually exclusive of each other?

    —Can you see the possibilities of balance in the divisions?

The examples of major divisions. You will need to master the mechanics of obtaining major divisions. Moreover, you will want to have qualitative divisions. We want to furnish examples of outlines.

(1) **Text:** Genesis 5:24

     Topic: The Best Exercise

     ETS: Enoch walked with God

     Proposition: You can walk with God.

     Objective: My objective is for my hearers to walk daily with God.

     Probing Question: What does it mean to walk with God?

     Unifying Word: *Meanings*

     Transitional Sentence: Let us notice some *meanings* of walking with God.

Outline:

    I. Walking with God means to go in God's direction.

   II. Walking with God means to proceed at God's pace.

 III. Walking with God means to progress as God leads.

 IV. Walking with God means to share God's companionship.

   V. Walking with God means to arrive at God's destination.

(2) **Text:** Mark 2:1-12

    Topic: The Miracle Worker

    ETS: Jesus helped a paralyzed man.

    Proposition: Jesus helps people with their needs.

    Objective: My objective is for people to experience Jesus' help in their lives.

    Probing Question: Why does Jesus help people?

    Unifying Word: *Reasons*

    Transitional Sentence: Let us observe some *reasons* why Jesus helps people.

Outline:

    I. Jesus wants to enhance your personhood.

   II. Jesus wants to give you a pardon.

 III. Jesus wants to give you a new possibility.

(3) **Text:** Ephesians 2:1-10 (Cited on page 90.)

(4) **Text:** James 1:19-26

    Topic: How to Use the Bible

    ETS: James taught Christians how to respond properly to God's Word.

    Proposition: We need to use the Bible correctly.

    Objective: My objective is to urge Christians to use the Bible according to God's instructions.

    Probing Question: How can you use the Bible correctly?

    Unifying Word: *Ways*

    Transitional Sentence: Let us notice some *ways* to use the Bible.

Outline:
    I. We can look into the Bible.
   II. We can listen to the Bible.
  III. We can live from the Bible.

(5) Text: Philippians 1:19-26
     Topic: Facing Your Death
     ETS: Paul faced the reality of his death.
     Proposition: Christians face death too.
     Objective: My objective is to prepare people for death.
     Probing Question: What happens when Christians face death?
     Unifying Word: *Observations*
     Transitional Sentence: Let us notice some *observations* about a Christian facing death.
     Outline:
    I. A Christian has an anxiety about death.
   II. A Christian has an answer for death.
  III. A Christian has an anticipation beyond death.

Expanding the Proposition

Having stated a proposition and having developed major divisions by using a probing question and a unifying word, you are now ready to use materials that give the message expansion. To enlarge or to expand the proposition, you will use substance material, including illustrations.

The use of substance material. You will need constant exposure to the sources of preaching material. Substance materials may be drawn from the following sources: Scripture, history, literature, personal observation and experience, imagination, biblical interpretation, and various other sources. Materials from these sources will be used in the following general ways: narrating, explaining, proving, applying, interpreting, and exhorting. These general methods function as means of giving substance to the sermon. Every piece of material and every general method of using the material will be used only as they relate to the questions, Does this material relate to the proposition? and will this material help to achieve my specific objective?

Now we are ready to share with you three specific ways of using substance material under the major divisions.

(1) A basic way to arrange substance material under each major division is to use the *textual analysis method.* This is a method which derives substance material from the text itself. You would profit from the study of the analysis of the text which is mentioned in chapter 2. The analysis of the text will help you expand the major divisions. You will select the matters which amplify major divisions, and you will also eliminate some of the analysis. Some texts lend themselves to the textual analysis method more readily than any other method of fashioning substance. Let us look at "God's Masterpiece" based on Ephesians 2:1-10 for an example of the textual analysis method.

Text: Ephesians 2:1-10

Topic: God's Masterpiece

ETS: Paul described Christians as God's workmanship.

Proposition: Christians are God's masterpieces.

Objective: My objective is to persuade people to allow God to shape their lives.

Probing Question: What does the text disclose about God's masterpiece?

Unifying Word: *Disclosures*

Transitional Sentence: Let us study the *disclosures* of the text about God's Masterpiece.

Outline:

I. God works with an impossible product. 2:1-3

    A. The lost person is dead in trespasses and sin. 2:1

    B. The lost person is dominated by the world, the devil, and the flesh. 2:2-3

II. God works with an incredible power. 2:4-6

    A. God's gracious character directs his power. 2:4

    B. God's great power raises the spiritually dead. 2:5-6

III. God works for an indomitable purpose. 2:7-10

    A. God wants to show his handiwork to the world. 2:7-9

    B. God wants his masterpiece to work. 2:10

The substance material under each major division came directly from the text.

(2) Another way to design substance material is to utilize the *facet method*. The major divisions will be expanded with various aspects in mind. This will be looking at every possible angle of each major division. Of course you will not use everything you think about but only those facets which help to expand the major divisions and to relate to people's needs. The facet method may be observed in the following sermon.

Text: Philippians 1:19-26
Topic: Facing Your Death
ETS: Paul faced the reality of his death.
Proposition: Christians face death too.
Objective: My objective is to prepare people for death.
Probing Question: What happens when Christians face death?
Unifying Word: *Observations*
Transitional Sentence: Let us notice some *observations* about a Christian facing death.
Outline:

    I. A Christian has an anxiety about death.

        A. New experiences bring a sense of anxiety.

        B. Leaving precious relationships causes anxiety.

    II. A Christian has an answer for death.

      A. Christians depend upon Christ's defeat of death.
      B. Christians will be raised because of Christ's resurrection.
  III. A Christian has an anticipation beyond death.
      A. Death does not end life for believers.
      B. Believers move into a richer, fuller life after death.

The substance material under each major division came as a facet of the division.

(3) Still another specific way of using substance material is to use *the text-today method.* Under each major division you will explain the meaning of the text, and then you will apply this meaning to the needs of people in today's world. Think of each major division supported by "then" material and "now" material. The sermon on "The Miracle Worker" is based on Mark 2:1-12 and is expanded as follows.

Text: Mark 2:1-12
Topic: The Miracle Worker
ETS: Jesus helped a paralyzed man.
Proposition: Jesus helps people with their needs.
Objective: My objective is for people to experience Jesus' help in their lives.
Probing Question: Why does Jesus help?
Unifying Word: *Reasons*
Transitional Sentence: Let us observe some *reasons* why Jesus helps people.
Outline:
    I. Jesus wants to enhance your personhood.
      A. Jesus valued a despised paralytic.
      B. Jesus values people whoever they are or whatever they have done.
   II. Jesus wants to give you a pardon.
      A. Jesus pardoned the paralytic.
      B. Jesus forgives sinners.

III. Jesus wants to give you a new possibility.
    A. Jesus gave the paralytic a new possibility.
    B. Jesus gives a new possibility.

The above three methods of designing substance material—textual analysis method, facet method, and text-today method—do not exhaust all the possible designs. We suggest that you begin with these methods, then you will be able to use other ways.

The use of illustrative material. Illustrations furnish profitable substance material for the sermon. Before you can use illustrations effectively, you need to understand the reasons for using them. Appropriate illustrations make ideas understandable, interesting, and persuasive. Let us notice briefly the reasons for using illustrations.

(1) Illustrations clarify abstract truths. They make ideas clear both to the preacher and to the audience. God's ideas can be communicated in pictorial form. Jesus used illustrations on many occasions and in various forms in order to clarify truths about the kingdom of heaven.

(2) Illustrations gain and keep people's interest. Beginning a sermon with an illustration arouses immediate attention. Using illustrations throughout the sermon helps hold the attention of the audience. Without a doubt James kept the attention of his hearers with illustrations. When he spoke of the Christian use of speech, he gave eight illustrations: bit in a horses' mouth; rudder on a ship; spark as cause of large fire; taming of beasts, birds, and reptiles; a spring; a fig tree; an olive tree; and salt water.

(3) Illustrations persuade people to act. When you make God's truths clear and interesting, people have a chance to respond. To conclude the Sermon on the Mount, Jesus used the illustration of the two houses, one built on the rock and the other built on the sand. By

using this illustration, he persuaded people to build their lives upon the rock.

The primary functions of illustrations are to explain, to interest, and to persuade. Of course other functions would be to aid memory, to give a break, to arouse emotions, and to give a transition. Do not use illustrations for illustration's sake. Learn their purpose and then incorporate them as material for your sermon.

Getting illustrations seems to be a continuous problem for preachers. With so many sermons to preach in a year, the securing of good illustrations will be a difficult task. Ian MacPherson in *The Art of Illustrating Sermons* suggests the following sources: the Bible, biographies, autobiographies, science, art, sculpture, newspapers, magazines, history, poetry, fiction, drama, general observation, and personal experiences. Enlarging your resources for illustration will help to ease the struggle of getting good illustrations for your sermon.

When you understand the purposes and resources of illustrations, you will be able to think about placing them in your sermon. Ideally speaking, you would be wise to use illustrative material at the beginning, throughout the major divisions, and in the conclusion. This would mean three to eight illustrations for each sermon. Illustrations do not have to be long. They may be quick insights or long stories. Perhaps the most effective use of illustrations is to get the attention of people in the introduction, to clarify the development periodically, and in the conclusion to persuade people to action. Nothing can help more in the expansion of a sermon than the wide and discriminating use of illustrations attractively communicated.

The purpose of structuring a sermon is to help people. Rather than just arranging points and subpoints, you will develop a proposition. You will put a probing question to the proposition. This will lead to an appropriate unifying word. The answers to the question will be fashioned with parallel statements, and they will be held together by a unifying word. The major divisions will be expanded with substance material and illustrations. Using these processes of structuring a sermon seems to function as a means of helping people.

Note

1. Clyde Fant, *Preaching for Today* (New York: Harper & Row Publishers, 1975), p. 135.

7
Introducing, Concluding, and Putting Transitions in the Sermon

The last phases of sermon construction are the introduction, the conclusion, and most of the transitions. Up to this point, preparing the sermon has put you through several stages. You started with a sermon idea either from a text or from a human need. Then you merged the biblical truth and the human need by getting an ETS and a proposition. You envisaged an audience, and you chose a specific objective. The proposition was probed, the unifying word chosen, and the major divisions were stated in parallel form. Also, substance materials and illustrations were selected.

Now you need to think about how to begin, to end, and to put transitions in the sermon. Ilion T. Jones said that the introduction and the conclusion were "the weakest parts of the average sermon."[1] Few homilists even discuss the matter of transitions. Introductions, conclusions, and transitions are far more than ornaments for the sermon-building process. Stopping short of thorough and careful preparation in these areas robs the sermon of communicative power and weakens the possibility of achieving your objective. In order to help with these matters, we shall consider introducing the sermon, concluding the sermon, and putting transitions in the sermon.

Introducing the Sermon

The importance of a good beginning for a sermon cannot be overemphasized. If the introduction fails, the whole sermon could be a lost cause. You need to study carefully the skills necessary in introducing a sermon. We shall seek to discover how introductions may be made to perform their functions.

The purposes of an introduction. Before you learn the art of introducing a sermon, you need to consider why a sermon needs an introduction. (1) You need an introduction in a sermon to get the attention of the audience. The introduction should act as a stimulant to make the listener want to hear what is to follow. You are simply trying to get the attention of your audience for an important sermon idea which is to be developed. Attention may be won or lost in the introduction.

(2) You need an introduction to build rapport with your audience. Your opening words will set listeners either for you or against you. Centuries ago, Aristotle, the Greek rhetorician, said that an introduction introduces the speaker as well as the speech. Securing immediate communion with an audience is important if we want them to hear God's message through us. If people detect instantly a kind, courteous, authentic, loving man of God, they will come nearer to listening attentively. The audience may decide you are the kind of person they can trust and want to hear. If the opening of a sermon reflects an arrogant, harsh, conceited, contentious person, the audience could develop a bias against anything you may say. Keep in mind that you introduce yourself as well as your subject.

(3) You need an introduction to present the basic sermon idea. The introduction should mention the proposition as skillfully and as quickly as possible. Presenting the proposition in the introduction helps the listeners understand the direction in which the sermon will move.

(4) You need an introduction to make clear the purpose of the sermon. With the introduction, you help people understand how the sermon relates to their lives. Consciously or unconsciously each listener asks, Why should I listen? What does this say to me? You need to make clear in the introduction how the sermon relates to people's needs.

(5) You need an introduction to make transition to the body of a sermon. The introduction helps to pave the way for the subject matter which is to follow. It avoids abruptness for both preacher and people. There seems to be audience delight in a gradual approach to the subject.

The qualities of an introduction. Since the introduction is so important, the distinctive qualities of a good introduction need to be examined. (1) A good introduction is of a suitable length. It will vary in length according to each sermon. Introductions will range in length from 2 to 10 percent of the sermon. An old woman once told John Owen, the Puritan preacher, that he was so long spreading the table that she lost her appetite for the meal.

(2) An introduction is suited for the particular sermon. Each introduction needs to be prepared for the sermon development which is to follow. Giving one direction of thought in the introduction and another direction of thought in the outline will confuse the audience. Prepare an introduction appropriate for the sermon.

(3) An introduction is simple, clear, and easy to follow. If the thoughts are too profound and the words too complicated, the people might be lost from the beginning. Seek to make the introductions as clear as possible.

(4) An introduction is interesting. You will seek to have an introduction which will interest your people. So, check to see if your introductions begin where people are.

The interrelated segments of an introduction. Now

we come to the important matter of what to put in an introduction. Having examined the purposes and qualities of introductions, you are now ready to learn three suggested segments of an introduction: attention-getting material, textual material, and relational material. The first segment of the introduction is the attention-getting segment. The best way to gain audience attention is to use a variety of interesting materials. The choice of materials are numerous and include: a life-situation experience, an incident from literature, a personal experience, a news item, a quotation, a statistic, a letter, a cartoon, a line of poetry, a hymn, a reference to a book, a case study, an excerpt from a conversation or a dialogue, a startling question, a humorous incident, or any other material which would gain the attention of the audience and would relate to the sermon idea. Think of the opening segment of your introduction securing the attention of your listeners.

The next segment for the introduction is the textual segment. Sermons ought to be based upon the Bible. The introduction is the logical place for the biblical basis of a sermon idea. Your study of the Bible which involved historical, analytical, and exegetical study will be most helpful. In this segment of the introduction, you could relate some pertinent historical or analytical information necessary for the people's understanding. Within this segment, the ETS needs to be stated as skillfully and as quickly as possible.

The final segment of the introduction is the relational segment. You will relate your text to the proposition and to the objective. Of course you will not *always* say, "My proposition is . . . ." and "My objective is . . . ." Most of the time the attention-getting material and the textual material will lead naturally to the use of the proposition and the objective. Both should flow naturally within this segment of the introduction. In addition to using the proposition and the objective, you will use a probing question and a unifying word. A transitional sentence which also uses the unifying word will lead you from introduction to the body of the sermon.

You need to remember that these three segments of an introduction are interrelated. You might think that these three segments will make the introduction too long. This does not have to be the case. Each segment, if prepared carefully, can fulfill its function, and you move swiftly to the sermon body.

An example of an introduction. Throughout the various processes of sermon preparation we have sought to give examples. We want to share an example of an introduction with the three segments.

Text: Philippians 1:19-26

Topic: Facing Your Death

ETS: Paul faced the reality of his death.

Proposition: Christians face death too.

Objective: My objective is to prepare people for death.

Probing Question: What happens when Christians face death?

Unifying Word: *Observations*

Transitional Sentence: Let us notice some *observations* about a Christian facing death.

Introduction:

1. Attention-Getting Segment

In George Seaton's film *The Proud and the Profane,* a young nurse goes to Iwo Jima where her husband had been killed during World War II. She goes to the cemetery where her husband was buried and turns to the caretaker, a shell-shocked soldier, who had seen her husband die. "How did he die?" she asked.

"Like an amateur," he replied. "They teach you how to hurl a grenade and how to fire a mortar, but nobody teaches you how to die. There are no professionals in dying!"

2. Textual Segment

Paul looked death in the face. He awaited the outcome

of his trial while he stayed in a Roman prison. From all indications death seemed inevitable. *He faced the reality of his death* (ETS). Our text gives an indication of how one great Christian, namely Paul, faced this matter of death.

3. Relational Segment

Every Christian inevitably faces the reality of death (ESS). According to Paul's insights we can have some interesting feelings about our death. *I want you to be as brave as possible and get ready to die* (Objective). What are some biblical observations that a Christian can make about death? (Probing Question). Using Paul's experiences, let us notice some *observations* a Christian can make about death.

Concluding the Sermon

The art of concluding a sermon will be a vital process in building sermons to meet people's needs. The importance of the conclusion cannot be overemphasized. Andrew W. Blackwood, a classical homilist, regarded the conclusion as "the most important part of a sermon, except for the text."[2] You will want to give careful attention to the matter of making conclusions effective.

The purposes of the conclusion. Before you learn the skills of concluding a sermon, you need to consider briefly the purposes of a conclusion. (1) A conclusion brings a sermon to an appropriate stopping place. Preparing a specific conclusion keeps you from meandering and searching for an effective close. You need to plan how to stop. The conclusion aids in planning the end before you come to it.

(2) A conclusion makes application of the main ideas which have been developed in the sermon body. In the conclusion, you need to make clear how the sermon idea applies to the hearers. Application will be found throughout the sermon, but special attention will be given to it in the conclusion.

(3) A conclusion helps to achieve the sermon objective. It will persuade people to act upon the truth in the sermon. No sermon is complete until you have challenged the hearers to act upon the message they have heard. The Holy Spirit brings this to pass, but the Spirit's work does not excuse you from preparing a conclusion which will persuade people to act.

(4) The conclusion helps to move the sermon to an invitation. Most authors on preaching deal with invitation as a separate segment; but since it is so closely linked with conclusion, we treat the invitation briefly at this point. You will want to realize that your conclusion leads to an invitation for a choice, an action, a commitment, a verdict on the part of the hearers.

The qualities of the conclusion. Having the purposes of a conclusion in mind, we shall be motivated to prepare the best conclusion for a sermon. What are the needful qualities of a conclusion? (1) A conclusion needs to be appropriate to that particular sermon. This is to say that the conclusion leads naturally out of the sermon body.

(2) A conclusion needs to be clear. The closing of a sermon is a time of conclusion not confusion.

(3) In most cases the conclusion needs to be brief. Its length will be determined by the nature of the sermon content and by the objective you desire to achieve. Practice word economy in the conclusion.

(4) The conclusion needs to be linked closely with the objective. This is a final opportunity for the essence of the sermon and for the sermon objective to be applied in order to meet people's needs.

(5) The conclusion needs to be personal. H. H. Farmer said that the conclusion "should have something of the quality of a knock on the door."[3]

(6) The conclusion needs to be positive. All the negative aspects belong to the body of the sermon. The conclusion should offer a positive hope.

(7) The conclusion needs to have the persuasive note.

It will have the "wooing note" of the Holy Spirit.

The interrelated segments of the conclusion. Just as we shared the interrelated segments of the introduction, we now call your attention to the interrelated segments of the conclusion. A beginning approach for preparing conclusions will be to design the conclusion with interrelated segments in mind. This is not the only way to design a conclusion, but it is a good way to begin. When you master these interrelated segments, you will devise other ways. The three segments will be the reproduction segment, the application segment, and the invitation segment.

The beginning of the conclusion will be the reproduction segment. In this segment you will seek to reproduce the essence of the sermon in a creative manner. This will be a summary of a truth just unfolded. The proposition can be rephrased in a single, brief, comprehensive statement that reproduces the truth of the entire discussion. So, the first segment of the conclusion will be a time to reproduce in a resumé fashion the thrust of the sermon.

After reproducing the essence of the sermon, you will move quickly to the application segment. This is the segment where you drive the truth home to the hearers. You can use all types of material to apply: incidents from life, episodes from literature, a news item, a conversation, a question or series of questions, an apt quotation, or others. You need to remember, though, that in the application segment you want to apply the truth to the hearers. You will persuade the hearers to accept the truth and do something about it. You will need to use the objective in this segment of the conclusion. Using it will help you to apply and to persuade for action.

The final segment of the conclusion will be the invitation segment. H. H. Farmer said that "a sermon has failed, indeed it has not been a sermon, unless it carries to the serious hearer something of a claim upon, or summons to, his will."[4] Your objective will determine the main emphasis of the conclusion. When the objective has been evangelistic, the invitation will be for people to repent and to open their lives to Jesus Christ. In addition to the invitation to accept Christ as Savior, you have three other types of invitation: to unite with the church; to decide for a deeper life; and to commit life to God's call to a particular vocation. You can possibly use all four types of invitations in a sermon, but the one linked with the objective will be given first and will be emphasized the most.

Remember that you are preparing a sermon to meet people's needs. Therefore, in the first segment of the conclusion, you will make the thrust of the sermon absolutely clear. In the second segment you will relate the sermon to the lives of people, and in the third segment you will close the sermon and invite people to take action.

An example of conclusions. To understand better the principles of concluding a sermon we shall give an example of a conclusion with three interrelated segments.

Text: Philippians 1:19-26
Topic: Facing Your Death
ETS: Paul faced the reality of his death.
Proposition: Christians face death too.
Objective: My objective is to prepare people for death.
Probing Question: What happens when Christians face death?
Unifying Word: *Observations*
Transitional Sentence: Let us notice some *observations* about a Christian facing death.
Conclusion:
1. The Reproduction Segment
Having to look at the fact of your death is not one of life's most pleasant activities. Nonetheless, the fact is certain that *Christians die too* (ESS). Observing some of

the biblical truths about the death of a Christian gives hope.

2. The Application Segment

You need to think seriously at this moment about your death. *I want you to get ready to die* (Objective). You need to make the proper preparation by opening your life to Jesus Christ. Believe me, believers can relate to Paul's observations about death.

3. The Invitation Segment

I want to say a word to nonbelievers. You need to think seriously about this matter of dying. I invite you to open your lives to Jesus Christ. That is the primary preparation for death. If you have opened your lives to Jesus Christ, you can share in the victory which the Lord gives. If nonbelievers receive Christ, I want you to acknowledge this publicly in our closing hymn.

Putting Transitions in the Sermon

An effective sermon should move from section to section with smoothness. Movement does not happen automatically. Therefore, think seriously about preparing transitions for the sermon. The word *transition* means "passing from one subject to another without abruptness." In a sermon a transition is the act of moving from one segment, point, division, and so forth of the sermon to another. There are three main transitions: from introduction to body; from major division to major division within the body; and from the body to the conclusion.

The values of transitions. Good transitions have several values which enhance the sermon. (1) Transitions save you from obscurity. Preparing transitions helps you to know how to move from place to place. Transitions will likely rescue hearers from being vague about your progression of thought.

(2) Transitions help test the unity of the sermon. This is especially true for the transitional sentence which is used to link the introduction to the major divisions. All

of the other transitions will be related somewhat to this first transitional sentence.

(3) Transitions contribute to the progress of the sermon. Ilion T. Jones said that "the sermon should make progress as it moves toward its conclusion."[5] When the movement of the sermon is interrupted, interest lags, minds wander, and attention can be lost. Transitions help move people from the beginning to the end of the sermon.

The types of transitions. Since a transition is so important, how does it happen? Several types could be utilized to move the sermon from one thought to another thought. (1) A prominent method is the relational type. One or more sentences could be used to show how each major division relates to the other major divisions. The sentence or sentences would all point directly or indirectly back to the proposition and to the unifying word. You may use the relational type transition as a mid-point sentence to look backward and to project forward. Let us use an example of a relational-type transition from "Facing Your Death." The following transition is from division I to division II: "So the Christian has an anxiety about death, but also the Christian has an answer for death." You will notice that the transitional sentence skillfully stated both the previous point and the subsequent point.

You may use the relational sentence to look only on one side. This means that either the previous or the subsequent material is stated but not both of them. Let us share an example: "The Christian has an anxiety about death, but this is not the only observation." The first division was stated, but the transitional implied the next division. Again, we notice: "This is one observation, but there is the observation that a Christian has an answer for death." In this example the first division was implied, and the second division was stated.

You may use the relational sentence as a transition

when neither the previous idea nor the subsequent idea is stated: "Facing death brings this observation, but there is another one." You would profit by mastering the relational-type transition.

(2) Another type of transition is the connecting-word-and-phrase type. Words and phrases can be used to link thoughts together. The most traditional type of word connection is: *first, second, third,* and so on; or *likewise, besides, moreover, furthermore, additionally, so, thus, for, because, since, whereas, next,* and many other words. You can also link thoughts with phrases such as: *in the next place, we also observe that, on the contrary, added to that, after that,* and other phrase combinations. You will help the movement and unity of your sermon by preparing these transitional words and phrases before you deliver the sermon.

(3) Another type of transition is the question type. This question is used to make transition, not to make the major divisions. The same question you used to probe the proposition could be used throughout to move from introduction to body, from major division to major division, and from body to conclusion. Asking a question leads naturally to an answer or another method of handling material in your sermon.

The examples of transitions. You can understand transitions better by studying examples. We shall give examples of the relational type, the connecting-word-and-phrase type, and the question type.

(1) The relational type
From introduction to body:
> How can we use the Bible properly? As we look at James 1:19-26, we shall notice some *ways* to use the Bible. The first way is obvious.

From major division to major division:
> I. We can look into the Bible, but we can also listen to the Bible.

    II. We can listen to the Bible, but there is another *way* to use the Bible.

   III. We can live from the Bible.

From body to conclusion:

We have looked at several *ways* to use the Bible. We have the instructions. Now we can apply these ways.

(2) The connecting-word-and-phrase type

From introduction to body:

What happens when Christians face the reality of death? Let us notice several *observations* which Paul made and which we also make.

From major division to major division:

    I. First, a Christian has an anxiety about death.

    II. In the next place, a Christian has an answer for death.

   III. Finally, a Christian has an anticipation beyond death.

From body to conclusion:

Indeed, Christians face death too! Consequently, we must face death with the biblical observations in mind.

(3) The question type

From introduction to body:

Why does Jesus help people? Let us notice some *reasons* Jesus helps.

From major division to major division:

    I. Jesus wants to enhance your personhood.

    II. Jesus wants to give you a pardon.

   III. Jesus wants to give you a new possibility.

From body to conclusion:

Now, we have some reasons Jesus helps people. Will you allow him to help you?

You must not stop short in constructing the sermon. Once the text has been studied or an idea emerges or once an idea has emerged from the people and linked with a suitable text, the sermon is not complete. It needs development and expansion. Oftentimes, a preacher thinks he is through when major divisions and substance materials have been prepared. No, building the sermon continues with introductions, conclusions, and transitions.

With the introduction, lead people to the sermon body by using attention-getting, connecting, and relational material. In the conclusion lead people from the essence of the sermon to action with the use of reproduction, application, and closing segments. Close hopefully and expectantly, and lean on the authority of God's Word and on the guidance and power of the Holy Spirit. Prepare to move the people from the beginning to the end of the sermon with relational sentences, connective words and phrases, or questions. Introductions, conclusions, and transitions do not just constitute sermon parts. They are functional in that they have a vital place in communicating God's truth to people.

Notes

1. Ilion T. Jones, *Principles and Practice of Preaching* (Nashville: Abingdon Press, 1956), p. 152.

2. Andrew W. Blackwood, *The Preparation of Sermons* (New York: Abingdon Press, 1948), p. 177.

3. H. H. Farmer, *The Servant of the Word* (Philadelphia: Fortress Press, 1942), p. 65.

4. Ibid.

5. Jones, p. 96.

8
Communicating the Sermon

The preacher studies and structures a sermon in order to get the message heard and heeded. No preacher, regardless of how skillfully he prepares a sermon, can expect the message to be received exactly as he intended. God's message comes through the human assimilation by the preacher, and it is received by the perception of a diversified audience. The real dilemma is to get God's message, which exists in the mind of the preacher, to the hearer with the greatest amount of understanding and the least amount of distortion. Granted this fact, you may observe readily that there would be no absolutely perfect communication. Since the matter of getting the message heard is so crucial, you will want to study and to practice the best in communication skills. You will want to study, prepare, and deliver the messages so that the audience may understand and heed them.

Communication of God's truth is not, and never has been, an option for the preacher. Learning the skills of getting God's message heard and heeded is imperative. Improving the skills of communicating a sermon will be studied by looking into the concept of communication, the preparation for communication, and the preacher as communicator.

The Concept of Communication

Before the preacher can communicate, he needs to understand some significant concepts of communication.

Communicating a sermon involves God's inspiration in preparation and delivery. God has chosen to deliver his divinely recorded message in the Bible through a human personality. Because preaching comes through human instrumentality, the latest studies in psychology and in behavioral sciences should be investigated. We shall investigate these concepts of communication and relate these ideas to preaching.

The definition of communication. Numerous theorists have proposed definitions of communication. Several definitions will be cited. Researchers at Yale University defined communication as "the process by which an individual (the communicator) transmits stimuli (usually verbal) to modify the behavior of other individuals (the audience)."[1] Merrill R. Abbey defines communication as "a process in which source and receiver interact more or less imperfectly in arriving at some degree of common understanding."[2] Reuel L. Howe affirms that communication occurs whenever there is a mutual "meeting of meanings."[3]

These definitions reflect a change in the concept of communication. For years the idea existed that communication involved the act of transmitting a message. It suggested something fixed or closed, as if a message passed from source to receiver. With this concept of communication, preaching was viewed as the bundling of ideas and then transmitting them to the congregation. This concept tended to make preaching a monologue where the preacher talked without keen awareness of the needs of people and with little effort to meet their needs.

Fortunately, progress in communication studies moved communication from a static, fixed model to one of interaction. The definitions of communication now involve the use of the word *process*. Some have been so excited by these new discoveries in communication that they have adopted verbal dialogue. Adopting the idea of communication as a process does not mean the congregation has to talk back. It means the preacher will seek to know people's needs and preach sermons for the purpose of meeting their needs. This would be a meeting of meanings. Edgar N. Jackson said, "In any relationship where there is no chance to talk back, there must be created a special atmosphere where persons can feel back."[4] You need to develop the art of understanding the needs of people, what they are thinking, and what their feelings are about the sermon at the time of delivery. Preaching then will be dialogical without the use of spoken words from the audience. It means a meeting of meaning, a creative interplay of minds between preacher and audience. It means a "feel back." The preacher and the congregation are caught up in a dynamic relationship in the preaching situation.

The factors in communication. To be a more effective communicator you need to be aware of the factors involved in the communication process. The four obvious factors in the communication process are the preacher, the message, the channel, and the audience.

(1) The first factor in communicating a sermon is the preacher. Numerous matters influence the preacher's effectiveness in communication. The intellectual, social, cultural, and religious elements will influence the building and communicating of your sermon. Your character is also involved. People will listen more readily to those they believe to be genuine. Your attitudes are involved. Do you feel good about yourself? Your attitudes color the process of communication. Furthermore, your knowledge of the Bible and your understanding of persons will enhance your success as a communicator. As a preacher of God's message you must encode your own thoughts and ideas into verbal and visual communication.

(2) The next factor in communication is the message. What passes between the preacher and the audience is a

message. The preacher must build a sermon, which contains an idea expressed in words and sentences, and transmit the sermon via verbal and nonverbal stimuli. Success in communication depends upon the harmonious blending of the verbal with the nonverbal—the vocal with the visual. You must have harmony between the verbal and the visual in your delivery. Success in communication is enhanced by using language (words and sentences) known to the audience. The goal is to share the biblical message in an understandable fashion.

(3) The third factor in the communication process is the channel. This is closely linked with the preacher. You use multiple channels to share your message with an audience: the spoken sermon, the nonverbal communication, and the setting where the sermon is preached. The message and the channel are inseparably bound together. The channel may either substantiate or oppose the message which you send. For example, you may speak on "Answers to Anxiety" with the channel of a worried facial expression, nervously fidgety gestures, and excessively high-pitch vocal tone. The message was designed as a therapy for anxiety, but the channel communicated anxiety. The words said one thing, but the visual channels said a different thing. Some communication experts such as Marshall McLuhan have said that the channel is the message. Whatever the opinion about that, you must seek harmony between the message and the channel.

(4) The fourth factor in the communication process is the audience. The hearers receive from a preacher an encoded message via a channel, and the hearers begin the process of decoding the message. Decoding is translating the visual, verbal, and physical stimuli into forms of internal response. Each hearer has a frame of reference and a realm of particular experience which help to select from the preacher whatever is of meaning. Skill, attitude, knowledge, religious background, and the

social-cultural system apply to the hearer. If you wish to communicate effectively, you must know the people to whom you preach. You must seek to ascertain the receiver's level of skills, attitudes, needs, religious background, and social-cultural system. When the receivers are given consideration, the act of preaching will become an interacting process rather than a preacher transmitting to a passive audience.

The Preparation for Communication

Communicating the sermon idea to people begins before the actual delivery of the sermon. You have to prepare yourself for communication with people. Getting an idea heard requires the preparation of yourself as well as the preparation of the sermon itself.

The preparation of the preacher. The essential business in preaching is not with sermon building but with preacher building. William A. Quayle said, "Preaching is the art of making a sermon and delivering it? Why, no, that is not preaching. Preaching is the art of preparing a preacher and delivering that."[5] A prepared preacher is needed to deliver the well-built sermon. You will need to prepare yourself to be an effective communicator.

How do you prepare yourself in order to communicate the gospel? An entire book could be written which deals with the personal preparation of the preacher. Ernest Mosley has written a book which describes the minister as one who preaches from his personhood. Mosley contends that for proclamation skills to improve, you must begin with your Christian character.[6] David Switzer in *Pastor-Preacher-Person: Developing a Pastoral Ministry in Depth* called preaching the sharing of oneself through words with other people. From his innermost being a preacher proclaims the Word of God. Having looked at this concept, we can proceed to learn how to prepare for communication. It starts with improving the person.

You may prepare to be a communicative person by scheduling regular communion with God. Spiritual preparation enhances your personhood. When you have spent time with God reading, studying, meditating, praying, brooding, reflecting, and listening, the audience will detect that you have been with God. An English lady once said to Alexander Whyte after his sermon, "Sir, you spoke as if you came straight from the court of the king." He responded, "Perhaps I did." In preparation for delivering a sermon, Whyte spent thirty minutes immediately prior to the service alone with God in prayer. The object of preaching is to meet some need of the people, and you will deliver with greater fidelity to that objective when you come to the hour of delivery fresh from intercession with God for the people and their needs. You can be a more effective communicative person by being God-conscious and by being people-conscious in the preparation and delivery of your sermon.

You may prepare to be a communicative person by encountering persons in the varied experiences of life. Personal contact with people produces knowledge of them and empathy for them. The communicative preacher perceives, senses, feels, and understands his hearers. You will gain understanding by listening to what they say about themselves, by observing their interpersonal relationships, by encountering them in family, work, and recreational episodes. Upon learning the persons who comprise your congregation, you will choose words and forms of presentation that your people can relate to and understand. The congregation is more capable of experiencing the message when they are in the process of understanding the person who seeks to preach God's Word.

You may prepare to be a communicative person by choosing to be in a continuous growth process. You will seek to grow in self-awareness and self-understanding. You will strive to have a good self-image and a healthy respect for people to whom you minister. You communicate how you feel about yourself to the audience. The audience also detects your feelings about them. Nothing could be of more value than for you to grow in understanding yourself as a person of worth as well as a fallible human being.

The preparation of the sermon. The making of a communicative person takes a lifetime, but the preacher cannot take that long with each sermon. The preacher must prepare with communication in mind. One could imagine that New Testament preachers prepared sermons in order to be heard. However, through the years the sermon moved from an oral medium to a written medium. Several years ago H. Grady Davis sought to help preachers prepare sermons with oral communication in mind. He called for preachers "to write for the ear."[7] He realized that many sermons had been prepared for the eye. Preachers had been taught to prepare solely with literary skills in mind. The use of manuscripts produced stiffness, impersonality, noninteraction, and disinvolvement of the preacher and his audience. Davis helped move preachers toward a more communicative style by asking them to write for the ear.

Clyde Fant has moved sermon preparation closer to oral communication with his concept of "the oral manuscript."[8] He contends that preachers should prepare their sermons in the medium in which they are to be delivered. The sermon is an oral communication, and it needs to be prepared in the oral medium. Writing a sermon tends to lead to the idea that a sermon is finished when the manuscript has been written. No, it has to be delivered, and if it has been prepared on paper it will be delivered orally. Perhaps to prepare orally would develop a communicative preparation style. The oral process of preparation results in an oral product for the oral medium of preaching.

How do you prepare a sermon orally? We shall con-

sider oral preparation in a series of stages. (1) The first
stage is the initial beginning of the sermon idea. The oral
preparation begins like the manuscript. You will study
the text carefully and make extensive exegetical notes.
You will then write on paper the text, topic, ETS, proposition, objective, probing question, unifying word, major
divisions, and substance material. This stage represents
a time of thinking through your sermon idea and writing
some notes.

(2) The second stage of the oral manuscript is the processing of your thoughts orally. With the written
thought of the sermon before you, you speak aloud the
introduction, using attention-getting material first,
textual material second, and connecting material third.
You will not try to be exact as you proceed with the first
oral attempt. You will try various angles of attention-
getting material, textual material, and connecting material before finalizing your introduction. You will need to
keep paper and pen handy to note briefly the key sentences which emerge.

When you have introduced the idea, you will proceed
to process orally the major divisions. In this way you will
develop the sermon idea in the medium in which it will
be delivered. The major divisions, substance material,
and illustrations will be processed orally. Time needs to
be taken to write brief records of your oral proceedings.
More than likely the initial wording and arrangement of
stage one will be altered during the oral processing in
stage two. The entire sermon idea might even take a
new direction with the oral processing. The initial written impressions of stage one will be clarified and refined
by the speaking process. Talking out the major divisions
and substance material helps you to hear the development before the audience hears it.

After speaking through the sermon body, prepare the
conclusion orally. Remember the three main segments of
a conclusion: reproduction segment, application seg-

ment, and the invitation segment. Speak through each one of these segments until you have heard the way you choose to conclude the sermon. As soon as you hear the way you want to conclude, write a few sentences on each part of the conclusion.

This stage is a rough oral draft of the sermon. You have heard a beginning for the sermon, the body of the sermon complete with support material and illustrations, and the ending of the sermon. Only a few sentences have been written. Most of the sermon has been externalized by speaking. Now you are ready for the final stage of oral preparation.

(3) The third stage of oral preparation is the recording of your oral thoughts on paper. The second stage has been a rough oral projection of the sermon with a few written notes. At this point you may study the notes and do some creative brooding over the oral process. Revise the major divisions or change the substance material if necessary. Work on the introduction and the conclusion by writing a few sentences. Now you are ready to talk the entire sermon aloud. The process will resemble the second stage except the third stage strives for more finality. In the final stage you will have spoken the sermon in much the same way that it will be delivered.

The oral process of preparation leads to the "oral manuscript." [9] The size of the oral manuscript will vary with different preachers. Some might involve a page or two. Others might want to make more extensive notes. Whatever the size of the oral manuscript, its purpose is to make a record of the preacher delivering the sermon before it is preached. The oral medium must be kept preeminent rather than the literary medium. Preparing the sermon orally enhances your ability to help people. Having prepared orally, you will enjoy more ease and freedom in the pulpit, for you are not talking about a subject as much as you are engaging in meaningful dialogue with your hearers. Preaching might become a real, meaningful encounter with people rather than the recitation of a speech before an audience. You can speak at least five to ten times faster than you can write. The oral preparation will conserve your time in sermon preparation.

The Preacher as Communicator

A sermon becomes a sermon when it is shared with an audience. Irrespective of how skillful the person is who prepares a proposition, an outline, substance material, and other segments of a sermon, if it is not communicated effectively to an audience, the effort will be worthless. A sermon represents a creative interaction of thought between a preacher and his people. When the structural parts of a sermon intermingle with the personality of the preacher, communication occurs. The preacher's skill as a communicator begins with his personality and proceeds to verbal and visual elements.

The preacher's self-communication. Whether you like it or not, you disclose yourself in delivery. Your personality and character will be viewed in the pulpit. Delivery begins not in the mouth or with the gestures but with your inner feelings. What the speaker is and feels as a person will be seen and heard through the channels of the eyes, face, body, voice, gestures, and posture. Communicating a sermon begins with a speaker's *being* and not his saying or doing. Whatever you *are* will ultimately be visual and vocal to an audience.

To enhance self-communication you need to possess a good attitude toward yourself, toward your audience, and toward your sermon. Your attitude toward yourself is reflected in delivery. Your like or dislike for self will show to hearers. You must learn to face and to accept yourself as a human being. A growing, healthy image of self-worth balanced with a confession of fallibility communicates an authentic person to an audience. A preacher with a good self-image neither talks down from an inflated image to people nor speaks negatively out of a deflated self-image.

As well as communicating a healthy self-image, you will communicate feelings toward your people. Favorable audience responses emerge when you have positive attitudes toward them. Consistent condemnation of people communicates an unhealthy attitude toward persons. Your task involves both diagnosis and therapy. Denunciatory preaching often issues from a person with a bad attitude, personal hostilities, and inner frustrations. Developing your God-given gift as a shepherd communicates to people that you are a caring person. Authentic shepherds love their sheep, seek to guide them, reprimand them when they stray, lead them in proper paths, take personal interest in the sheep, and demonstrate understanding.

You also communicate your character in sermon delivery. Søren Kierkegaard gave a principle of communication when he said, "Only one transformed by Christianity can teach Christianity." Personal integrity is basic for a spokesman for God. Listeners hear character. They detect truthfulness, honesty, unselfishness, and sincerity. Character communicates. Not everyone can understand words and sermon arrangement, but every one understands Christian character. Nothing can enhance you as a communicator more than allowing the Holy Spirit to produce character in your life.

The preacher's vocal communication. Communicating the sermon proceeds from *being* to saying and doing. Working on character alone will not suffice. You must work on using properly your God-given voice. God expects the maximum possibilities from the voice. To achieve the voice potential, you need to understand the mechanics of voice production. Dwight E. Stevenson and Charles F. Diehl give four activities involved in the oral speech process: respiration, phonation, resonation, and articulation.[10] We shall not discuss these matters in detail. Instead, we suggest that a careful study of Stevenson and Diehl be made.

(1) Respiration is the act of breathing. Breath gets the speech underway. There are two kinds of breathing—one for biological needs and the other for speech. Normal breathing is involuntary and proceeds primarily from the chest and upper part of the body. Breathing for speaking should not be in the upper part of the body. Instead, it should be diaphragmatic or abdominal. Breathing for speaking has to differ because air will have to be inhaled quickly and quietly. You will need to keep a supply of air in the lungs for proper phrasing and projection. The diaphragm is a powerful muscle dividing the thorax from the abdomen. By its action it pushes air silently from the lungs. Diaphragmatic breathing eliminates constriction at the vocal chords and surrounding resonators. It also affects projection, rate, pitch, and poise.

You need to develop the art of diaphragmatic breathing when you preach. Stevenson and Diehl give clear instructions for attaining this type of breathing.[11] One simple way to discover whether your diaphragm is being used is to put one hand on the chest and the other on the abdomen. If diaphragmatic breathing occurs the abdomen will move forward, while the chest remains passive.

(2) Phonation is the production of sound. Breath passes through the vocal chords in the larynx, and sound occurs. The God-given length and thickness of the vocal chords determines the pitch of a voice. For this reason preacher's voices vary from high pitch to low pitch. God uses all types of voice pitches to communicate his message.

Each person has a normal pitch sound. Stevenson and Diehl call this "one's optimum pitch."[12] Your optimum pitch can be discovered with the use of a piano. You can sing down the scale to the lowest note that you can sustain comfortably. Then you will go up five keys. That tone usually represents your normal speech pitch. If you cannot sing, the optimum pitch level may be discovered by lying down, and when comfortably relaxed, vocalizing the "ah" sound almost as a sigh. This sound will be the optimum pitch.

When you discover your optimum pitch, you can use it for more effective speaking. You can have a greater range from normal to higher or lower sounds. The preacher who has a wide range and uses it habitually will be more interesting than one whose range is limited to a monotone. Inflecting sounds also enhances verbal communication. Stevenson and Diehl give four types of inflections: downward, upward, circumflex, and flat. These are used in the following ways: downward, for strong affirmation; upward, for questions; circumflex, for a variety of mixed emotions like doubt and sarcasm; and flat, for disappointment or disgust.[13] You will want to utilize your normal pitch level and to work on variation of your voice.

(3) Resonation is the amplification and reinforcement of sound in the cavities of the throat, nose, head, and mouth. Proper use of the resonating chambers give tonal quality to the voice. By understanding and using the human resonators efficiently, the voice quality can be improved greatly. Failing to use resonators properly will lead to nasality, breathiness, and harshness. Nasality occurs either because oral sounds come through the nose or because no sound comes through the nasal passages. Breathiness happens when too much uncontrolled air escapes. This results in a half-whisper and half-voice. Harshness occurs when there is excessive tension and constriction in the throat and mouth.

(4) Articulation is the formation of vowel and consonant sounds by the use of the tongue, teeth, and lips. To communicate effectively you must study constantly

the art of shaping sounds into words. Enunciating properly means that people hear audibly what you are saying.

There are roughly fifty different sounds in American speech. Stevenson and Diehl say that these sounds may be misarticulated in four ways: (1) omitted sounds, as in *Misipi* (Mississippi); (2) distorted sounds as in *Jeesus* (Jesus); (3) substituted sounds, as in *Chicargo* (Chicago); and (4) added sounds, as in *idear* (idea).[14]

You can improve your ability to articulate. First develop flexibility in your tongue, lips, and jaw muscles. Second educate your powers of hearing so that faults with your articulation can be heard and corrected. Third, study phonetic manuals and work constantly on all sounds of American speech.[15]

Now with a degree of understanding of voice production, you should learn about voice control. You command the volume, rate, variations, and vigor of your voice. First, you control the volume. Volume increases by expelling more air from the diaphragm, and it decreases by limiting the amount of air expelled. You will need to project enough to be heard but not enough to offend the listeners. You need to learn to project the right volume by your diaphragmatic thrust.

Second, you determine your rate of speaking. The rate will vary according to each preacher's personality. Rate is defective only if it is so rapid that it hinders understanding, or if it is so slow that it produces boredom. At times in delivering the sermon you will want to increase the rate, while at other times in the same sermon you will want to decrease the rate of delivery. Pausing occasionally will help in sermon delivery.

Third, you control variety in your voice. Flexibility should be exercised in rate, projection, and emphasis. Vocal monotony could constitute a real problem. Variety in every area of vocal production will prevent monotony.

Fourth, you determine the vigor of the voice. Actually

the volume, rate, and variety figure in to the energy of the voice. People listen to a speaker who seems to be interested and involved in his subject. You will want adequate control over volume, rate, and variations. When you have that control, you convey a dynamic personality.

The preacher's visual communication. To be a convincing preacher you must consider visual effectiveness as well as vocal effectiveness. You carry your body with you into the pulpit, and how you handle it proves either to be an asset or a liability. How you use nonverbal communication indicates your personality. As we consider the communication of a sermon, we need to ask what the preacher says by his appearance, his posture, his facial expression, his gestures, and his body movements.

Visual communication needs to coincide with vocal communication. Your action needs to match your words. One of the great hindrances in communication is when the preacher delivers two sermons at the same time, one vocally and a contrasting one visibly. Thomas M. Scheidel said that "a speaker's word may show strength, whereas his posture reveals weakness; the unsteady hand and the lack of eye contact may say more than the sentences spoken."[16] When the visual and the vocal messages are in opposition to each other, the hearers must choose which meaning to accept as the true intent of the preacher.

Effective visual communication depends upon your personality. You cannot prepare for visual communication, for this comes from inward motivation. Visual communication emerges out of an inner impulse to get an idea across to others. When you feel deeply about a sermon, and you desire others to act on the sermon, you will use your body as a natural part of communicating the idea. Facial expressions, gestures, and eye contact emerge from your mental attitude toward your people and their needs. The most impressive visual communication involves expressive action, and you should be conscious of the significance of this as a communication skill.

You can plan many segments of the sermon, but you cannot plan visual communication. It happens by the natural use of the body. How then can you enhance your ability to communicate visually? First, establish and keep eye contact with the hearers. Focusing the eyes in the direction of the audience speaks of your desire to communicate. Good eye contact encourages audience attention. Second, avoid attempting to plan gestures. The lifting of an eyebrow, the smile or frown on your face, the shrugging of a shoulder, the clinching of a fist, the pointing of a finger, the waving of an arm, and other movements come to life from within you. When gestures are planned, artificiality results. Third, allow body movements to happen by your involvement with the subject and with the audience. If your sermon moves toward a humorous slant, you will respond with a smile. Likewise, if it moves in the direction of a tragedy, you will have a serious countenance. Involvement with the subject matter in the sermons leads to spontaneous, appropriate body movement.

Getting a sermon heard involves a crucial part of preaching. Your desire should be to build and to deliver a sermon so that you may help people with their needs. If people are to hear and heed your sermon, you will need to work continuously on your character and spiritual life, on your verbal skills, and on your visual factors. Our hearts, minds, voices, and bodies go into communicating sermons.

Building sermons to meet people's needs does not come in one class, in reading a few books, or in natural gifts. Building and delivering sermons to meet people's needs requires God's gift of preaching and a lifetime of praying, thinking, studying, reading, meditating, and listening. We wish you God's best on your pilgrimage toward more effective preaching.

Notes

1. "Procedures and Effects of Mass Communication," *Mass Media and Education*, ed. Nelson B. Henry (Chicago: University of Chicago Press, 1954), p. 113.

2. Merrill R. Abbey, *Communication in Pulpit and Parish* (Philadelphia: The Westminster Press, 1973), p. 24.

3. Cf. Reuel L. Howe, *The Miracle of Dialogue* (New York: The Seaburg Press, 1963).

4. Edgar N. Jackson, *A Psychology for Preaching* (New York: Hawthorn Books, Incorporated, 1961), p. 64.

5. William A. Quayle, *The Pastor-Preacher* (New York: Eaton & Mains, 1910), p. 368.

6. See Ernest Mosley, *Priorities in Ministry* (Nashville: Convention Press, 1978).

7. H. Grady Davis, *Design for Preaching* (Philadelphia: Fortress Press, 1058), p. 265.

8. Clyde Fant, Preaching for Today (New York: Harper & Row Publishers, 1975), pp. 118-126.

9. Ibid., pp. 121-124.

10. Dwight E. Stevenson and Charles F. Diehl, *Reaching People from the Pulpit: A Guide to Effective Sermon Delivery* (New York: Harper & Row Publishers, 1958), pp. 16-17.

11. Ibid., pp. 40-48.

12. Ibid., p. 20

13. Ibid., pp. 22-23.

14. Ibid., pp. 28-29.

15. Ibid., pp. 28-35.

16. Thomas M. Scheidel, *Persuasive Speaking* (Glenview, Illinois: Scott, Foresman, & Company, 1967), p. 54.

Conclusion

A Checklist for Building Sermons to Meet People's Needs

1. Am I ready to begin building this sermon?
   A. Do I know, love, and want to help these people?
   B. Do I accept the biblical text as the inspired, authoritative Word of God?
   C. Is my life at this moment yielded to the guidance of the Holy Spirit?
   D. Am I ready to give my best in study and in preparation of this sermon?
2. Is the idea for this sermon biblically based and people-oriented? Does it measure up to the qualities of a good sermon idea?
3. Is the essence of the text (ETS) accurately, clearly, and succinctly stated? If so, have I studied, thought, and prayed over the text?
4. Is my proposition, the essence of the sermon (ESS), true to the text, related to a need of my people, and concisely stated in the present or future tense?
5. Is my objective to expose a truth and no more, or is it to change or to strengthen a life by exposing this truth?
6. Is my probing question to the proposition the proper one for dealing with the needs of people? Should it be *what*? — Should it be *why*? — Should it be *how*?
7. Is my unifying word the ideal plural word that will

cause all major divisions to be linked closely with it?

8. Are my major divisions stated in complete sentences in the present or future tense? Is each independent and at the same time tied together by the unifying word to guarantee oneness for the body of the sermon? Are these divisions expressed in parallel form?

9. Is there appropriate and adequate explanation, narration, and illustration in the body of the sermon to make it clear and convincing to the people?

10. Is the introduction attention getting, and does it introduce this sermon to the hearers?

11. Is the conclusion so stated as to persuade people to act favorably on the objective?

12. Is the invitation related directly to the objective of the sermon?

13. Am I aware that this sermon is not my work alone but that really it is the work of the Holy Spirit in and through me?

14. And now as I prepare to deliver this sermon do I come to the people with love for God and them, do I come with awareness of the fact that this is a message from God's Word designed to meet their need?

Now as you continue in the guidance and power of the Holy Spirit you can come to the pulpit to proclaim the Word of God in boldness, in power, and in love.

"And now, Lord, look upon their threats, and grant to thy servants to speak thy word with all boldness. . . . And when they had prayed, the place in which they were gathered together was shaken; and they were all filled with the Holy Spirit and spoke the word of God with boldness" (Acts 4:29,31, RSV).

Bibliography

Abbey, Merrill R. *Communication in Pulpit and Parish.* Philadelphia: Westminster Press, 1973.

Abbey, Merrill R. *The Word Interprets Us.* Nashville: Abingdon Press, 1967.

Armstrong, James. *Telling Truth: The Foolishness of Preaching in a Real World.* Waco: Word Books, 1977.

Baumann, J. Daniel. *An Introduction to Contemporary Preaching.* Grand Rapids: Baker Book House, 1972.

Best, Ernest. *From Text to Sermon: Responsible Use of the New Testament in Preaching.* Atlanta: John Knox Press, 1978.

Blackwood, Andrew W. *Expository Preaching for Today: Case Studies of Bible Passages.* Nashville: Abingdon Press, 1953.

Blackwood, Andrew W. *Planning A Year's Pulpit Work.* Grand Rapids: Baker Book House, 1942.

Blackwood, Andrew W. *The Preparation of Sermons.* Nashville: Abingdon Press, 1948.

Black, James. *The Mystery of Preaching.* Grand Rapids: Zondervan Publishing House, 1924.

Broadus, John A. *On the Preparation and Delivery of Sermons.* Rev. ed. Vernon L. Stanfield. San Francisco: Harper and Row, Publishers, 1979.

Browne, Benjamin. *Illustrations for Preaching.* Nashville: Broadman Press, 1977.

Brown, H. C., Jr. *A Quest for Reformation in Preaching.* Waco: Word Books, Publishers, 1968.

Brown, H. C., Clinard, H. Gordon, and Northcutt, Jesse J. *Steps to the Sermon: A Plan for Sermon Preparation*. Nashville: Broadman, 1963.

Cleland, James T. *Preaching to be Understood*. Nashville: Abingdon Press, 1965.

Cox, James W. *A Guide to Biblical Preaching*. Nashville: Abingdon Press, 1976.

Craddock, Fred B. *As One Without Authority*. Nashville: Abingdon Press, 1979.

Craddock, Fred B. *Overhearing the Gospel*. Nashville: Abingdon Press, 1978.

Davis, H. Grady. *Design for Preaching*. Philadelphia: Fortress Press, 1958.

Demaray, Donald E. *An Introduction to Homiletics*. Grand Rapids: Baker Book House, 1974.

Demaray, Donald E. *Proclaiming the Truth: Guides to Scriptural Preaching*. Grand Rapids: Baker Book House, 1979.

Erdahl, Lowell O. *Preaching for the People*. Nashville: Abingdon Press, 1976.

Fant, Clyde E. *Preaching for Today*. New York: Harper & Row, Publishers, 1975.

Fisher, Wallace E. *Who Dares to Preach? The Challenge of Biblical Preaching*. Minneapolis: Augsburg Publishing House, 1979.

Ford, D. W. Cleverley. *The Ministry of the Word*. Great Britain: William B. Eerdmans Publishing Company, 1979.

Gilmore, Alec. *Tomorrow's Pulpit*. Valley Forge: Judson Press, 1975.

Hall, Thor. *The Future Shape of Preaching*. Philadelphia: Fortress Press, 1971.

Howe, Reuel L. *The Miracle of Dialogue*. New York: The Seabury Press, 1963.

Jackson, Edgar N. *A Psychology for Preaching*. New York: Hawthorn Books, Inc., 1961.

Jackson, Edgar N. *How to Preach to People's Needs*. Grand Rapids: Baker Book House, 1972.

Jensen, Richard A. *Telling the Story: Variety and Imagination in Preaching.* Minneapolis: Augsburg Publishing House, 1980.

Jones, Ilion T. *Principles and Practice of Preaching: A Comprehensive Study of the Art of Sermon Construction.* Nashville: Abingdon Press, 1956.

Koller, Charles, W. *Expository Preaching Without Notes Plus Sermons Preached Without Notes.* Grand Rapids: Baker Book House, 1962.

Luccock, Harford E. *Communicating the Gospel: The Lyman Beecher Lectures of Preaching, 1953 Yale University.* New York: Harper & Brothers, Publishers, 1954.

McLaughlin, Raymond W. *The Ethics of Persuasive Preaching.* Grand Rapids: Baker Book House, 1979.

MacPherson, Ian. *The Art of Illustrating Sermons.* Nashville: Abingdon Press, 1964.

Massey, James Earl. *The Responsible Pulpit.* Anderson, Indiana: Warner Press, 1974.

Massey, James Earl. *The Sermon in Perspective: A Study of Communication and Charisma.* Grand Rapids: Baker Book House, 1976.

Miller, Donald G. *The Way to Biblical Preaching: How to Communicate the Gospel in Depth.* Nashville: Abingdon Press, 1957.

Mitchell, Henry H. *The Recovery of Preaching.* San Francisco: Harper & Row, Publishers, 1977.

Pattison, T. Harwood. *The Making of the Sermon.* Philadelphia: The American Baptist Publication Society, 1898.

Pearce, J. Winston. *Planning Your Preaching.* Nashville: Broadman Press, 1967.

Sangster, W. E. *The Craft of Sermon Construction.* Philadelphia: Westminster Press, 1951.

Sleeth, Ronald E. *Proclaiming the Word.* Nashville: Abingdon Press, 1964.

Steimle, Edmund A., Niedenthal, Morris J., and Rice, Charles L. *Preaching the Story.* Philadelphia: Fortress Press, 1980.

Sweazey, George E. *Preaching the Good News.* Englewood Cliffs: Prentice-Hall, Inc., 1976.

Switzer, David K. *Pastor, Preacher, Person: Developing a Pastoral Ministry in Depth.* Nashville: Abingdon Press, 1979.

Teikmanis, Arthur L. *Preaching and Pastoral Care.* Englewood Cliffs: Prentice-Hall, Inc., 1964.

Ward, Wayne E. *The Word Comes Alive.* Nashville: Broadman Press, 1969.

White, R. E. O. *A Guide to Preaching.* Grand Rapids: William B. Eerdmans Publishing Company, 1973.